Unlocking the Supernatural Power of Prayer

by Robert Rite

Table of Contents

Dedication

Get Complimentary Access to: "Prophecy Alerts"

Dear Reader: Prophecies are being fulfilled so
rapidly in these last days that I am offering my
readers complimentary access to "*prophecy alerts*"
so that you get "*Breaking Prophecy News*" as soon
as it breaks...Just follow this link below and sign Up
today...
http://robertritebooks.com/prophecy-alerts/

Dedication

To my Mom who has sacrificed her life to raise her children in the best manner possible.

I dedicate this book to you Mom this day, which is Mother's Day, and which also happens to be your birthday! *What a testament to how special a person you are.*

For all the years of wonderful memories, love, compassion, and kindness - **thank you**!

Your impact on my life, and all those who have been blessed by your warm heartedness, is your legacy. God Bless you!

Chapter 1 - Does God Really Listen to Our Prayers?

If my people who are called by my name, will humble themselves, and pray and seek my face, and turn from their wicked ways, then I will hear from heaven, and will forgive their sin, and heal their land."
2 Chronicles 7:14

If food can heal the body, then prayer can heal the mind, body and soul! Many believers have suffered needlessly because they do not know how to pray in the correct manner. Others complain that they never seem to receive answers to their prayers. This book was written because I want to share with you how countless tragedies can be avoided in life through consistent prayer. God has already empowered us with the greatest blessing of all - the incredible supernatural power of prayer!

The bible is God's handbook for mankind. In it is all the wisdom that we will ever need to live an abundant life full of God's blessings and favor.

Prayer is powerful because, when we believe, the spoken word can become reality. Our w**ords can manifest themselves into the physical realm, so we must pray wisely**.

Prayer is what gets us saved, and that alone is a testament to how powerful words and prayer are! God creates miracles and blessings through our prayers.   God changes the fate of man and nations through the prayers of the faithful. Did you know that every word that we pray is recorded in Heaven forever! We read this in the following passage**:**

Revelation 8:3

"Then another angel, having a golden censer, came and stood

*at the altar. He was given much incense that he should offer it **with the prayers of all the saints** upon the golden altar which was before the throne."*

As I explained in my book **"Bible Verses for Supernatural Blessings",** when we pray, we should cite specific passages related to whatever it is that we are praying for. *If we learn to harness the Power of Prayer, prayer can change any circumstance. Prayer can heal the sick, heal your finances, and it can do anything that is good for you.*

The Privilege of Prayer

We should thank God every day for the privilege of prayer. Prayer is a blessing and a privilege. Prayer is what gets us saved, and that alone is a testament to how powerful prayer is! God creates miracles and blessing through our prayers. God changes the fate of man and of nations through the prayers of the faithful. Nations have been restored and blessed through the prayers of their citizens. And every word that we pray is recorded in Heaven forever (Revelation). Jesus our Lord, said that if we had the faith of a mustard seed, then we could move mountains.

If it is good and in accordance with the laws of God, whatever we pray and bind on Earth will be done. If we learn to harness the Power of Prayer, prayer can change any circumstance. It is our God given right for us to communicate one on one with the our Creator!! What an awesome, powerful weapon and blessing.

God listens when we pray for our leaders and nation. Throughout history, nations and peoples have been restored and blessed through the prayers of its citizens. We read this promise in the following passage:

2 Chronicles 7:14:

"If my people who are called by my name, will humble themselves, and <u>pray</u> and seek my face, and turn from their wicked ways, then I will hear from heaven, and will forgive their sin, and heal their land."

We learn from the bible that ***<u>nothing in the kingdom of God operates without Faith, love or Patience</u>***. Without Faith, Love, and Patience, we cannot receive answers to our prayer(s); because our prayers will be just insincere words - and any chance of these words reaching God's ears will be short circuited by the lack of sincerity of heart.

Be positive in your thinking. Do not allow past failures, negative images, or doubt (worries) to interfere with your prayer time. Instead *meditate on positive results. Even before you receive them*, you must believe and boldly claim your victory over the mountain(s) that you confront.

We need the whole armor of God (**Ephesians 6:13**) to overcome in this earth, which **includes prayer**, and the word of God among other key things. Prayer is what keeps us focused on what matters in this life - an intimate relationship with God.

James 4:7 tells us to resist the devil and he will flee (run with fear) from us. The devil fears wise Christians who know the word and know who they are (children of Almighty God). We must resist doubt as it is from the devil. **1 Peter 5:8** Tells us to be sober (alert) against evil because he constantly searches for a home inside a non-believer. Prayer strengthens us so that we can resist the devil and his temptations.

In **Mathew Ch. 4 Vs. 7** the Devil even tempted Jesus at his weakest point (during a 40 day fast). *Like a roaring lion, the enemy will always attack you at your weakest point, so that is the area of our life that we must guard and protect the most with fervent prayer*!

Make every prayer a statement of faith. Thank God before you receive it believing wholeheartedly that you will - and you will!

Why do Bad things happen to Good People?

It is not our fault when bad things happen to us. That is the price we all have to pay at times for being a member of the human race, and subject to the curse of sin. However, as I will explain now, the bible clearly reveals that mankind was not placed on earth to be subject to the whims of chance, suffering and misfortune.

Our Authority here on Earth

We have been given much "authority" while here on earth. Let's review what the bible reveals about our authority.

We can Pray with Authority

The following passage explains the authority that God gave us: Genesis Ch 1 vs. 26 "Let us create man in our image after our likeness; let them have dominion……over all the earth"…..and he gave us dominion/authority over the Earth (like God has dominion in heaven). God authorized us to have dominion over all the earth. Dominion is the power of governing and controlling, power to direct, control, use and dispose at our pleasure. We are in charge and control the affairs of this planet.

We are responsible for what happens in our earth and our lives! We are in charge and therefore responsible, because God gave us the Authority to control to direct our lives in this earth.

God's word and promises in the Bible is his will so when we are praying for healing or anything else that is righteous, we do not need to pray like this: *"Lord if it is your will…."*. If it is good for our soul and in accordance with the word than it is God's will, period!

8 Key Principals we learn from Genesis Ch 1 vs. 26:

1) The legal authority to dominate earth has been given to mankind only. Neither Demons, nor angels, and nothing else has this authority!

2) God did not include himself (during the age of man) in the legal authority over the earth.

3) Man became the legal steward over planet earth.

4) Man is a spirit with a physical body and we rule the earth - *that is why Jesus had to be born in a physical body to save mankind!*

5) A spirit without a body is illegal in the earth. This is why the Holy Spirit can only dwell inside of us.

6) Any influence or interference from the supernatural here on earth can only manifest itself by permission of man (**through _prayer_**). Only **we can authorize** Godly or Demonic interference and or influence in our lives; **only WE can!**

7) God Himself who is a spirit without a physical body made himself subject to this law (the law of man's exclusive authority on earth). This is why we see throughout the bible, that God performed His works exclusively through men like Noah, Abraham, Moses, King David, St. Paul and others. Of course he is God and in total control (he gives us the breath of life and the heartbeat and he can take it away at will). So we cannot do anything good without God, but God cannot do great works on earth without a man/woman – at least not for these 6000 years that he has given us dominion.

8) Satan also is subject to this law of authority as well. This is why original sin had to manifest itself through the **_willful_** actions of Adam and Eve. Throughout this age we witness all of the evils on earth being perpetrated by leaders of nations like Herod, Hitler, Stalin, and a host of individuals who have committed atrocities throughout this age. Certainly, Satan can influence and eventually corrupt man's soul so that he commits all kinds of atrocities, but man will be held

accountable because man has the authority to say **"NO"** to Satan and sin.

That answers the question as to why God seems to allow so many atrocities to occur without His direct intervention. God needs our prayers - our authority to intervene in our lives.

So, because of God's **_integrity he cannot intervene without our authorization, because we are earth's legal authority (yes, even over Satan, demons, and principalities). God never breaks a promise or his word. He cannot because he is perfect._**

Through proper and fervent prayer we can apply the authority that God blessed mankind with, when He created us. Heaven needs license, which is our authority, in order to perform works and miracles in our life. Our authority through our prayers is that license!

Chapter 2 - Prayer Basics

*In this manner, therefore, pray: "Our Father in heaven, Hallowed be Your
name.*
*Your kingdom come. Your will be done On earth as it is in heaven. Give us
this day our daily bread.*
*and forgive us our debts, as we forgive our debtors. And do not lead us
into temptation,*
*But deliver us from the evil one. For Yours is the kingdom and the power
and the glory forever. Amen."*
Matthew 6:9-17

The Lord's Prayer (**Mathew 6:9**) is just an outline, so we
should not limit ourselves to reciting this prayer. We cannot
expect miracles and answers by just reciting the "Our Father";
although it could form a portion of our prayer session. This is
why Jesus said "***in this manner, therefore pray***". For
example, the right prayer should start with worshiping God,
just like in the Lord's Prayer. So, we can use it as an outline -
but we should translate it into our own words. God gave us all
the gift of creativity or at least a measure thereof. So we
should structure our prayer specific to our situation.

Your Prayer Life should….

1) Be built and established upon the word of God.

2) Be **specific** and stand on God's word. Find the verse
   in the Bible that specifically covers what you are
   praying for. I.e. for healing find healing versus (such as
   Psalm 30:2; Psalm 107:20**; Isaiah 53:5; Mathew 8:8;
   Proverbs 4:20-22).** Direct your prayers to God. Ask
   God for the thing you want and believe that you

received it. **Mathew Ch 6 Vs. 32** God knows what we need before we ask; but we have to ask.

3) <u>Be positive in your thinking</u>. Do not allow failure, negative images or doubt to enter your mind (worrying). Instead meditate on positive results. **James 4:7** tells us to ***resist the devil and he will flee (run with fear) from us***. The devil fears knowledgeable Christians who know the word and know who they are (children of the Lord). We must resist doubt as it is from the devil. **1 Peter 5:8** Tells us to be sober (alert) against evil because he searches for a home inside a non-believer. **Ephesians 6:13**: We need the whole armor of God to overcome in this earth, includes praying, the word of God among other key things. In **Mathew Ch. 4 Vs. 7** the Devil even tempted Jesus in his weakest point (during a 40 day fast).

4) <u>Guard your mind</u>. **2 Corinthians 10:5** tells us we have the authority/power to cast down wrong thinking and negative thoughts.

5) <u>Meditate on God's promises</u>. **Joshua Ch. 1 vs. 8;** we should ***meditate on the word*** day and night to keep evil away, and for any other needs or wants. Meditate until the word speaks to you (through the peace of God). Jesus meditated on the word of God constantly, and he is our example (since he is our Heavenly Father). **Proverbs 4:20-22** shows us that meditating on the word provides life and health! **John 15:7** promises that if we abide in the word, ask what you desire and it shall be done.

6) <u>Continually thank God for the answer.</u> **1 Thesalonians 5:18** says that in all things we must give thanks, for that is the will of God. **Deuteronomy 28:47** tells us we must serve our God with joy and *gladness of heart.* **Phiippians 4:6** tells us to make our requests/prayers with *thanksgiving.* We need an attitude of gratitude just like the saints in heaven **Revelations 11:17.** That is how they made it there! <u>Hint:</u> *so we should read Revelations carefully and copy all the prayers and songs of the elders, saints and the 4 living creatures in Heaven!*

7) <u>Make every prayer a statement of faith.</u> Thank God before you receive it knowing that you will; and you will!

Prayer is our tool for divine intervention. <u>Prayer unlocks the authority that we have been given by God the almighty</u>!

Prayer is……

1) Man giving God legal right to interfere in earths/our affairs.
2) Man giving heaven earthy license to influence earth.
3) Prayer is terrestrial (earthly) license for celestial interference
4) Man using his/her legal authority to invoke heavens influence on the planet and our lives.
5) Great things happen for people who pray.

Rules to Praying

1) <u>Pray to the father in the name of Jesus</u>. **John Ch. 16 Vs. 23-24**

(ask and you will receive). Always pray to the Father God in Jesus name. It is Jesus who gives us the authority to approach the Father. Jesus makes intersession for all of us because we are all mortal sinners unworthy to speak directly to the Almighty. **All of our authority flows through Jesus since no one has any standing in Heaven except Jesus as disclosed in the book of Revelations**. Prayers that are not prayed in the name of Jesus will not be heard in Heaven. Our prayers are answered in Jesus name.

2) <u>Believe that you will receive when you pray</u>. You need to believe that you already received it when you pray for something**. If you "hope" you will receive it then you might not because you did not "believe" it in your heart**. Many prayers get cancelled because we did not believe that our prayer would be answered – it is that simple! Read **Mark Ch. 11 vs. 24; Hebrews 11:6; 2 Corinthians Ch. 5 Vs. 7**

3) <u>Forgive others if you want prayer to work</u>. Prayers can't be answered if we have un-forgiveness in our heart. As the Lord's prayer says "…forgive us our sins as we forgive those who sin against us. **Mark Ch 11 Vs. 24-26; Mathew 5:24**

4) <u>Depend on the Holy Spirit to help us pray wholeheartedly</u>.

5) <u>Understand how the Holy Spirit will help us in intercession and supplication</u>.

6) <u>Don't pray to be seen by others</u>. Pray in secret lest you be like the hypocrites Jesus cited in **Mathew 6:5**. Instead pray in secret, and God who sees in secret will reward openly. Prayer is between just God and us.

7) <u>God responds to faith and not to much speaking or many words</u>. **Mathew 6:7** Don't think you will be heard by many words or vain repetitions. You will not be heard for many words or recitals but by your faith.

8) <u>Put the Kingdom of God First</u>. In other words, pray for spiritual blessings - not earthly blessings.

9) <u>Pray in the name of Jesus</u>. **John Ch 16 Vs. 23.** Jesus clearly instructs us that upon his death we are NOT to ask him anything. But rather we are to *ask God in the name of Jesus* and God will hear our prayer.

Consequences of NOT Praying

1. God cannot intervene in our lives for our benefit, unless we authorize him (thru prayer).
2. We are at the mercy of all of the evils, demons and principalities in this world.
3. We become disconnected from God, and all of his blessings.

Chapter 3 - Examples of Powerful Prayers from the Bible

*"Be joyful always; **pray continually**; give thanks in all circumstances, for this is God's will for you in Christ Jesus."* **1 Thessalonians 5:16-18**

The following are great prayers by great men of God (including from the Messiah Himself). These prayers are not placed in the bible to demonstrate their holiness, but rather to teach and impress upon us how we should pray, and the importance and power of prayer. Note how most of these prayers are *intimate heartfelt conversations with the Lord* rather than bland recitals or repetitious blurbs that are not meaningful, heartfelt or sincere.

Moses (an early picture of Jesus) Prayed and interceded for his People

Moses is an early example of Jesus Christ who intercedes for us in heaven. Moses was a very humble man, and the ONLY man whom God spoke face to face with. He managed to successfully lead and put up with several million rebellious Jews for over 40 years in the harshest of conditions; in their journey throughout the Sinai Desert. Like Jesus, Moses bore the burdens and the sins of his people and I believe that is why he was not allowed to enter the Promised Land. His level of character and leadership was all but supernatural. Among God's Old Testament patriarchs, Moses is my most favorite hero. By the way, there are many great men of God in the bible that we can aspire to be like. Notwithstanding, I am truly humbled by the greatness of this man - Moses.

Thanks to Moses, under Gods guidance, despite their many transgressions, the children of Israel did make it to

the Promised Land. As Christians, we all journey through the dry desert of life (for around 40 years after adulthood). Along the way there are many setbacks. As we transgress, we repent and we get back up, and we struggle to set our moral compass back on track. Just like our Jewish brothers, trials and tribulations is the cross that we all must bear in this side of heaven. But through strong prayer, faith and perseverance we too can make it to the Promised Land!

Moses interceded more than once for his people. It changed God's mind about destroying the rebellious children of Israel who repeatedly provoked God to anger. This is a great example of how we can intercede for others through prayer - and how God listens to our heartfelt prayers.

Numbers 14:13-20

"And Moses said to the Lord: "Then the Egyptians will hear it, for by Your might You brought these people up from among them, 14 and they will tell it to the inhabitants of this land. They have heard that You, Lord, are among these people; that You, Lord, are seen face to face and Your cloud stands above them, and You go before them in a pillar of cloud by day and in a pillar of fire by night. 15 Now if You kill these people as one man, then the nations which have heard of Your fame will speak, saying, 16 'Because the Lord was not able to bring this people to the land which He swore to give them, therefore He killed them in the wilderness.' 17 And now, I pray, let the power of my Lord be great, just as You have spoken, saying, 18 'The Lord is longsuffering and abundant in mercy, forgiving iniquity and transgression; but He by no means clears the guilty, visiting the iniquity of the

fathers on the children to the third and fourth generation. **¹⁹** *Pardon the iniquity of this people, I pray, according to the greatness of Your mercy, just as You have forgiven this people, from Egypt even until now."* **²⁰ Then the Lord said: "I have pardoned, according to your word**;"

Below we read how Moses once again intercedes for the children of Israel:

Exodus 32:9-14

9 **And the Lord said to Moses**, *"I have seen this people, and indeed it is a stiff-necked people! 10 Now therefore, let Me alone, that My wrath may burn hot against them and I may consume them. And I will make of you a great nation."*

11 Then Moses pleaded with the Lord his God, and said: **"Lord, why does Your wrath burn hot against Your people whom You have brought out of the land of Egypt with great power and with a mighty hand? 12 Why should the Egyptians speak, and say, 'He brought them out to harm them, to kill them in the mountains, and to consume them from the face of the earth'? Turn from Your fierce wrath, and relent from this harm to Your people. 13 Remember Abraham,**

Isaac, and Israel, Your servants, to whom You swore by Your own self, and said to them, 'I will multiply your descendants as the stars of heaven; and all this land that I have spoken of I give to your descendants, and they shall inherit it forever." 14 **So the Lord relented from the harm which He said He would do to His people**.

And as if this was not enough, just like Messiah Jesus Christ, Moses was willing to give up his life (in his case - eternal life) by having God blot him out of the **Book of Life** for the sins of the children of Israel!

Exodus 32:31-33

"Then Moses returned to the Lord and said, *"Oh, these people have committed a great sin, and have made for themselves a god of gold!* 32 **Yet now, if You will forgive their sin—but if not, I pray, blot me out of Your book which You have written."**

33 And the Lord said to Moses, "Whoever has sinned against Me, I will blot him out of My book.

King David's Prayers

The following prayers are examples as to why God referred to King David as *"a man after His heart"*. Despite being a courageous warrior, King David was a kind,

humble, gentle, and righteous man. Several generations later - from the seed of King David, would be born another humble, gentle, and righteous man by the name of Jesus Christ. Among many titles, Christ is also referred to as "the root and the offspring of David, The bright and morning star". Like David, He also will be a great warrior when He returns to earth as the "King of Kings and Lord of Lords"!

Although one of the greatest warriors in the bible, king David was blessed with other gifts. Like his creator God, King David was blessed with an incredible gift of creativity (he was also a great harpist). King David spoke and wrote some of the greatest psalms, prayers, and songs recorded in the bible (read Psalms). His son Solomon would also inherit that same gift of writing (Solomon wrote Ecclesiastes, Proverbs, and the Songs of Solomon).

King David's Prayer for Forgiveness

Below, King David offers us a perfect prayer that we can pray for our transgressions.

To the Chief Musician. A Psalm of David when Nathan the prophet went to him, after he had gone in to Bathsheba.

"Have mercy upon me, O God,
According to Your loving kindness;
According to the multitude of Your tender mercies,
Blot out my transgressions.
² Wash me thoroughly from my iniquity,
And cleanse me from my sin.

³ For I acknowledge my transgressions,
And my sin is always before me.

23

⁴ Against You, You only, have I sinned,
And done this evil in Your sight—
That You may be found just when You speak,
And blameless when You judge.
⁵ Behold, I was brought forth in iniquity,
And in sin my mother conceived me.
⁶ Behold, You desire truth in the inward parts,
And in the hidden part You will make me to know wisdom.
⁷ Purge me with hyssop, and I shall be clean;
Wash me, and I shall be whiter than snow.
⁸ Make me hear joy and gladness,
That the bones You have broken may rejoice.
⁹ Hide Your face from my sins,
And blot out all my iniquities.
¹⁰ Create in me a clean heart, O God,
And renew a steadfast spirit within me.
¹¹ Do not cast me away from Your presence,
And do not take Your Holy Spirit from me.
¹² Restore to me the joy of Your salvation,
And uphold me by Your generous Spirit.
¹³ Then I will teach transgressors Your ways,
And sinners shall be converted to You.
¹⁴ Deliver me from the guilt of bloodshed, O God,
The God of my salvation,
And my tongue shall sing aloud of Your righteousness.
¹⁵ O Lord, open my lips,
And my mouth shall show forth Your praise.
¹⁶ For You do not desire sacrifice, or else I would give it;
You do not delight in burnt offering.
¹⁷ The sacrifices of God are a broken spirit,
A broken and a contrite heart—
These, O God, You will not despise.

King David is the perfect example of gratitude, humility, kindness - and as we read in 2 Samuel, he knew how to praise and worship the Lord.

2 Samuel 7:18-29

Then King David went in and sat before the Lord; and he said:

"Who am I, O Lord God? And what is my house, that You have brought me this far? 19 And yet this was a small thing in Your sight, O Lord God; and You have also spoken of Your servant's house for a great while to come. Is this the manner of man, O Lord God? 20 Now what more can David say to You? For You, Lord God, know Your servant. 21 For Your word's sake, and according to Your own heart, You have done all these great things, to make Your servant know them. 22 Therefore You are great, O Lord God.[a] For there is none like You, nor is there any God besides You, according to all that we have heard with our ears. 23 And who is like Your people, like Israel, the one nation on the earth whom God went to redeem for Himself as a people, to make for Himself a name—and to do for Yourself great and awesome deeds for Your land—before Your people whom You redeemed for Yourself from Egypt, the nations, and their gods? 24 For You have made Your people Israel Your very own people forever; and You, Lord, have become their God.

25 "Now, O Lord God, the word which You have spoken concerning Your servant and concerning his house, establish it forever and do as You have said. 26 So let Your name be magnified forever, saying, 'The Lord of hosts is the God over Israel.' And let the house of Your servant David be established before You. ²⁷ For You, O Lord of hosts, God of Israel, have revealed this to Your servant, saying, 'I will build you a house.' Therefore Your servant has found it in his heart to pray this prayer to You.

²⁸ "And now, O Lord God, You are God, and Your words are true, and You have promised this goodness to Your servant. ²⁹ Now therefore, let it please You to bless the house of Your servant, that it may continue before You forever; for You, O Lord God, have spoken it, and with Your blessing let the house of Your servant be blessed forever."

David's Prayers were like Poetry

King David is credited for writing many if not most of the Psalms. Just before he retired his kingship, David prayed the following which reads more like beautiful poetry and a song full of heartfelt love and adoration. Note how prayer does not have to be boring! God gave us all tremendous creative capacity to express ourselves before Him with loving words, songs and worship. The following is a perfect example.

2 Samuel 22:2-51

"The Lord is my rock and my fortress and my deliverer;
³ The God of my strength, in whom I will trust;
My shield and the horn of my salvation,
My stronghold and my refuge;
My Savior, You save me from violence.
⁴ I will call upon the Lord, who is worthy to be praised;
So shall I be saved from my enemies.
⁵ "When the waves of death surrounded me,
The floods of ungodliness made me afraid.
⁶ The sorrows of Sheol surrounded me;
The snares of death confronted me.
⁷ In my distress I called upon the Lord,

And cried out to my God;
He heard my voice from His temple,
And my cry entered His ears.
⁸ "Then the earth shook and trembled;
The foundations of heaven[b] quaked and were shaken,
Because He was angry.
⁹ Smoke went up from His nostrils,
And devouring fire from His mouth;
Coals were kindled by it.
¹⁰ He bowed the heavens also, and came down
With darkness under His feet.
¹¹ He rode upon a cherub, and flew;
And He was seen[c] upon the wings of the wind.
¹² He made darkness canopies around Him,
Dark waters and thick clouds of the skies.
¹³ From the brightness before Him
Coals of fire were kindled.
¹⁴ "The Lord thundered from heaven,
And the Most High uttered His voice.
¹⁵ He sent out arrows and scattered them;
Lightning bolts, and He vanquished them.
¹⁶ Then the channels of the sea were seen,
The foundations of the world were uncovered,
At the rebuke of the Lord,
At the blast of the breath of His nostrils.
¹⁷ "He sent from above, He took me,
He drew me out of many waters.
¹⁸ He delivered me from my strong enemy,
From those who hated me;
For they were too strong for me.
¹⁹ They confronted me in the day of my calamity,
But the Lord was my support.
²⁰ He also brought me out into a broad place;
He delivered me because He delighted in me.
²¹ "The Lord rewarded me according to my righteousness;
According to the cleanness of my hands
He has recompensed me.
²² For I have kept the ways of the Lord,

And have not wickedly departed from my God.
23 For all His judgments were before me;
And as for His statutes, I did not depart from them.
24 I was also blameless before Him,
And I kept myself from my iniquity.
25 Therefore the Lord has recompensed me according to my righteousness,
According to my cleanness in His eyes.[d]
26 "With the merciful You will show Yourself merciful;
With a blameless man You will show Yourself blameless;
27 With the pure You will show Yourself pure;
And with the devious You will show Yourself shrewd.
28 You will save the humble people;
But Your eyes are on the haughty, that You may bring them down.
29 "For You are my lamp, O Lord;
The Lord shall enlighten my darkness.
30 For by You I can run against a troop;
By my God I can leap over a wall.
31 As for God, His way is perfect;
The word of the Lord is proven;
He is a shield to all who trust in Him.
32 "For who is God, except the Lord?
And who is a rock, except our God?
33 God is my strength and power,[e]
And He makes my[f] *way perfect.*
34 He makes my[g] *feet like the feet of deer,*
And sets me on my high places.
35 He teaches my hands to make war,
So that my arms can bend a bow of bronze.
36 "You have also given me the shield of Your salvation;
Your gentleness has made me great.
37 You enlarged my path under me;
So my feet did not slip.
38 "I have pursued my enemies and destroyed them;
Neither did I turn back again till they were destroyed.
39 And I have destroyed them and wounded them,
So that they could not rise;

They have fallen under my feet.
40 For You have armed me with strength for the battle;
You have subdued under me those who rose against me.
41 You have also given me the necks of my enemies,
So that I destroyed those who hated me.
42 They looked, but there was none to save;
Even to the Lord, but He did not answer them.
43 Then I beat them as fine as the dust of the earth;
I trod them like dirt in the streets,
And I spread them out.
44 "You have also delivered me from the strivings of my people;
You have kept me as the head of the nations.
A people I have not known shall serve me.
45 The foreigners submit to me;
As soon as they hear, they obey me.
46 The foreigners fade away,
And come frightened from their hideouts.
47 "The Lord lives!
Blessed be my Rock!
Let God be exalted,
The Rock of my salvation!
48 It is God who avenges me,
And subdues the peoples under me;
49 He delivers me from my enemies.
You also lift me up above those who rise against me;
You have delivered me from the violent man.
50 Therefore I will give thanks to You, O Lord, among the Gentiles,
And sing praises to Your name.
51 "He is the tower of salvation to His king,
And shows mercy to His anointed,
To David and his descendants forevermore."

King Solomon Prayed for the Right thing

The following prayer (again it is more like intimate conversation) is a great example of how when we pray for the right thing the lord may bless us beyond our expectations. King Solomon prayed just for wisdom to judge righteously, and God blessed him with much, much more as we read…

1 Kings 3:4-14

4 Now the king went to Gibeon to sacrifice there, for that was the great high place: **Solomon offered a thousand burnt offerings** *on that altar.* *5 At Gibeon* **the Lord** *appeared to Solomon in a dream by night; and God said, "Ask! What shall I give you?"*

6 And Solomon said: "You have shown great mercy to Your servant David my father, because he walked before You in truth, in righteousness, and in uprightness of heart with You; You have continued this great kindness for him, and You have given him a son to sit on his throne, as it is this day. 7 Now, Oh Lord my God, You have made Your servant king instead of my father David, but I am a little child; I do not know how to go out or come in. 8 And Your servant is in the midst of Your people whom You have chosen, a great people, too numerous to be numbered or counted. 9 **Therefore give to Your servant an understanding heart to judge Your people, that I may discern between good and evil. For who is able to judge this great people of Yours**?"

*10 **The speech pleased the Lord**, that Solomon had asked this thing. 11 **Then God said to him:** "Because you have asked this thing, and have not asked long life for yourself, nor have asked riches for yourself, nor have asked the life of your enemies, but have asked for yourself understanding to discern justice, 12 behold, I have done according to your words; see, I have given you a wise and understanding heart, so that there has not been anyone like you before you, nor shall any like you arise after you. 13 And I have also given you what you have not asked: both riches and honor, so that there shall not be anyone like you among the kings all your days. 14 So if you walk in My ways, to keep My statutes and My commandments, as your father David walked, then I will lengthen your days."*

Daniel's Prayer

Note: This powerful prayer would not only lead to the Israelite's release from captivity, but also led to a visitation from the **Arch-angel Gabriel** on more than one occasion - who would reveal to Daniel events that would take place in the end of this age (the time we are living in now).

Daniel 9:4-20

And I prayed to the Lord my God, and made confession, and said,
"O Lord, great and awesome God, who keeps His covenant and mercy with those who love Him, and with those who keep His commandments, 5 we have sinned and committed iniquity, we have done wickedly and rebelled, even by departing from Your precepts and Your judgments. 6 Neither have we heeded Your servants the prophets, who spoke in Your name to our

31

kings and our princes, to our fathers and all the people of the land. *7* O Lord, righteousness belongs to You, but to us shame of face, as it is this day—to the men of Judah, to the inhabitants of Jerusalem and all Israel, those near and those far off in all the countries to which You have driven them, because of the unfaithfulness which they have committed against You.

8 "O Lord, to us belongs shame of face, to our kings, our princes, and our fathers, because we have sinned against You. *9* To the Lord our God belong mercy and forgiveness, though we have rebelled against Him. *10* We have not obeyed the voice of the Lord our God, to walk in His laws, which He set before us by His servants the prophets. *11* Yes, all Israel has transgressed Your law, and has departed so as not to obey Your voice; therefore the curse and the oath written in the Law of Moses the servant of God have been poured out on us, because we have sinned against Him. *12* And He has confirmed His words, which He spoke against us and against our judges who judged us, by bringing upon us a great disaster; for under the whole heaven such has never been done as what has been done to Jerusalem.

13 "As it is written in the Law of Moses, all this disaster has come upon us; yet we have not made our prayer before the Lord our God, that we might turn from our iniquities and understand Your truth. *14* Therefore the Lord has kept the disaster in mind, and brought it upon us; for the Lord our God is righteous in all the works which He does, though we have not obeyed His voice. *15* And now, O Lord our God, who brought Your people out of the land of Egypt with a mighty hand, and made Yourself a name, as it is this day—we have sinned, we have done wickedly!

16 "O Lord, according to all Your righteousness, I pray, let Your anger and Your fury be turned away from Your city Jerusalem, Your holy mountain; because for our sins, and for the iniquities of our fathers, Jerusalem and Your people are a reproach to all those around us. 17 Now therefore, our God, hear the prayer of Your servant, and his supplications, and for the Lord's sake cause Your face to shine on Your sanctuary, which is desolate. 18 O my God, incline Your ear and hear; open Your eyes and see our desolations, and the city which is called by Your name; for we do not present our supplications before You because of our righteous deeds, but because of Your great mercies. 19 O Lord, hear! O Lord, forgive! O Lord, listen and act! Do not delay for Your own sake, my God, for Your city and Your people are called by Your name."

Jesus Prayed

Just before He was crucified, Jesus prayed the following prayer for His disciples and for their seed (the body of Christ, the Christian church). The perfect prayer by the perfect man.

John 17: Jesus spoke these words, lifted up His eyes to heaven, and said:

"Father, the hour has come. Glorify Your Son, that Your Son also may glorify You, 2 as You have given Him authority over all flesh, that He should[a] give eternal life to as many as You have given Him. 3 And this is eternal life, that they may know You, the only true God, and Jesus Christ whom You have sent. 4 I have glorified You on the earth. I have finished the work which You have given Me to do. 5 And now, O Father,

glorify Me together with Yourself, with the glory which I had with You before the world was.

⁶ "I have manifested Your name to the men whom You have given Me out of the world. They were Yours, You gave them to Me, and they have kept Your word. ⁷ Now they have known that all things which You have given Me are from You. ⁸ For I have given to them the words which You have given Me; and they have received them, and have known surely that I came forth from You; and they have believed that You sent Me.

⁹ "I pray for them. I do not pray for the world but for those whom You have given Me, for they are Yours. ¹⁰ And all Mine are Yours, and Yours are Mine, and I am glorified in them. ¹¹ Now I am no longer in the world, but these are in the world, and I come to You. Holy Father, keep through Your name those whom You have given Me,[b] that they may be one as We are. ¹² While I was with them in the world,[c] I kept them in Your name. Those whom You gave Me I have kept;[d] and none of them is lost except the son of perdition, that the Scripture might be fulfilled. ¹³ But now I come to You, and these things I speak in the world, that they may have My joy fulfilled in themselves. ¹⁴ I have given them Your word; and the world has hated them because they are not of the world, just as I am not of the world. ¹⁵ I do not pray that You should take them out of the world, but that You should keep them from the evil one. ¹⁶ They are not of the world, just as I am not of the world. ¹⁷ Sanctify them by Your truth. Your word is truth. ¹⁸ As You sent Me into the world, I also have sent them into the world. ¹⁹ And for their sakes I sanctify Myself, that they also may be sanctified by the truth.

20 "I do not pray for these alone, but also for those who will[e] believe in Me through their word; 21 that they all may be one, as You, Father, are in Me, and I in You; that they also may be one in Us, that the world may believe that You sent Me. 22 And the glory which You gave Me I have given them, that they may be one just as We are one: 23 I in them, and You in Me; that they may be made perfect in one, and that the world may know that You have sent Me, and have loved them as You have loved Me.

24 "Father, I desire that they also whom You gave Me may be with Me where I am, that they may behold My glory which You have given Me; for You loved Me before the foundation of the world. 25 O righteous Father! The world has not known You, but I have known You; and these have known that You sent Me. 26 And I have declared to them Your name, and will declare it, that the love with which You loved Me may be in them, and I in them."

Like Jesus demonstrated when he raised Lazarus from the dead, if you have great faith and **pray as if you have already received the answer** - you can manifest great miracles for yourself and others.

John 11:41-44

""Father, I thank You that You have heard Me. 42 And I know that You always hear Me, but because of the people who are standing by I said this, that they may believe that

You sent Me." *43 Now when He had said these things, He cried with a loud voice, "Lazarus, come forth!"* 44 And he who had died came out bound hand and foot with grave clothes, and his face was wrapped with a cloth. Jesus said to them, "Loose him, and let him go."

The Lord's Prayer

Matthew 6:9-13

"You, therefore, pray like this:

'Our Father in heaven!
May your Name be kept holy.
May your Kingdom come,
your will be done on earth as in heaven.

Give us the food we need today.
Forgive us what we have done wrong,
as we too have forgiven those who have wronged us.
And do not lead us into hard testing,
but keep us safe from the Evil One.
For kingship, power and glory are yours forever."

Moving Mountains (Trials) through Effective Prayer

When You Pray with Faith You can move Mountains.

David and Goliath

David's courage, faith and bold declaration, allowed him to easily kill the giant Goliath - even though David was barely armed. Like David, we must understand that we should not fear the battles or the mountains that we face in life, when we allow the Lord to fight our battles for us.

1 Samuel 17:42-47

42 And when the Philistine looked about and saw David, he disdained him; for **he was *only* a youth**, ruddy and good-looking. **43** So the Philistine said to David, "*Am* I a dog, that you come to me with sticks?" And the Philistine cursed David by his gods.**44** And the Philistine said to David, "Come to me, and I will give your flesh to the birds of the air and the beasts of the field!"

45 Then David said to the Philistine, ***"You come to me with a sword, with a spear, and with a javelin. But I come to you in the name of the Lord of hosts, the God of the armies of Israel, whom you have defied. 46 This day the Lord will deliver you into my hand, and I will strike you and take your head from you. And this day I will give the carcasses of the camp of the Philistines to the birds of the air and the wild beasts of the earth, that all the earth may know that there is a God in Israel. 47 Then all this assembly shall know that the Lord does not save with sword and spear; for the battle is the Lord's, and He will give you into our hands."***

Hezekiah's Prayer Extended His Life by 15 years

Even the impossible can become reality when we approach the Lord the right way. Hezekiah's prayer changed God's mind and he was granted 15 more years of life! So even when it's your time to meet the maker, God will listen to your intercessory prayer.

2 kings 20:1-7

*"In those days **Hezekiah was sick and near death**. And Isaiah the prophet, the son of Amos, went to him and said to him, **"Thus says the Lord: 'Set your house in order, for you shall die, and not live.'"***

*² **Then he turned his face toward the wall, and prayed to the Lord, saying, ³ "Remember now, O Lord, I pray, how I have walked before You in truth and with a loyal heart, and have done what was good in Your sight." And Hezekiah wept bitterly.***

*⁴ And it happened, before Isaiah had gone out into the middle court, that the word of the Lord came to him, saying, ⁵ "Return and tell Hezekiah the leader of My people, 'Thus says the Lord, the God of David your father: **"I have heard your prayer, I have seen your tears; surely I will heal you.** On the third day you shall go up to the house of the Lord. ⁶ **And I will add to your days fifteen years**. I will deliver you and this city from the hand of the king of Assyria; and*

I will defend this city for My own sake, and for the sake of My servant David."'

⁷ Then Isaiah said, "Take a lump of figs." So they took and laid it on the boil, and he recovered."

Nehemiah Prays for his Nation and his People

As he hears of the suffering of the returning exiles, Nehemiah gives an example of how to pray for a nation, and its people, and for deliverance from any circumstances that we may face.

Nehemiah 1:4-11

⁴ So it was, when I heard these words, that I sat down and wept, and mourned *for many* days; I was fasting and praying before the God of heaven.

And I said: *"I pray, Lord God of heaven, O great and awesome God, You who keep Your covenant and mercy with those who love You and observe Your[c] commandments,⁶ please let Your ear be attentive and Your eyes open, that You may hear the prayer of Your servant which I pray before You now, day and night, for the children of Israel Your servants, and confess the sins of the children of Israel which we have sinned against You. Both my father's house and I have sinned. ⁷ We have acted very corruptly against You, and have not kept the commandments, the statutes, nor the ordinances which You*

*commanded Your servant Moses.⁸ Remember, I pray, the
word that You commanded Your servant Moses, saying,
'If you are unfaithful, I will scatter you among the
nations;⁹ but if you return to Me, and keep My
commandments and do them, though some of you were cast
out to the farthest part of the heavens, yet I will gather them
from there, and bring them to the place which I have chosen
as a dwelling for My name.'¹⁰ Now these are Your servants
and Your people, whom You have redeemed by Your great
power, and by Your strong hand.¹¹ O Lord, I pray, please let
Your ear be attentive to the prayer of Your servant, and to the
prayer of Your servants who desire to fear Your name; and let
Your servant prosper this day, I pray, and grant him mercy in
the sight of this man."*

Hannah Prays that she may bear a Child

1 Samuel 1

"Lord Almighty, if you will only look on your servant's misery
and remember me, and not forget your servant but give her a
son, then I will give him to the Lord for all the days of his life,
and no razor will ever be used on his head."

The Criminal's Words on the Cross, saved his Soul

If even the thief on the cross could receive salvation, how
much more can anyone receive eternal life when in sincerity of
heart they repent and acknowledge the true Lord and savior -
just as the thief on the cross demonstrated.

Luke 23:40-43

But the other, answering, rebuked him, saying, *"Do you not even fear God, seeing you are under the same condemnation?* [41] *And we indeed justly, for we receive the due reward of our deeds; but this Man has done nothing wrong."* [42] *Then he said to Jesus, "Lord, remember me when You come into Your kingdom."*
[43] *And Jesus said to him, "Assuredly, I say to you, today you will be with Me in Paradise."*

Pray with a Thankful Spirit

Mary's Prayer of Thankfulness - Mary, the mother of Jesus, demonstrates how to pray with a thankful spirit:

Luke 1:46 - 49

"My soul doth magnify the Lord, and my spirit has rejoiced in God my Savior. For he has regarded the low estate of his handmaiden; for behold, from henceforth all generations shall call me blessed. For He that is mighty has done to me great things; holy is His name."

A Prayer of Rejoicing

Habakkuk 3:2-19

"O Lord, I have heard Your speech *and* was afraid;
O Lord, revive Your work in the midst of the years!
In the midst of the years make *it* known;
In wrath remember mercy.

³ God came from Teman,
The Holy One from Mount Paran. *Selah*
His glory covered the heavens,
And the earth was full of His praise.
⁴ *His* brightness was like the light;
He had rays *flashing* from His hand,
And there His power *was* hidden.
⁵ Before Him went pestilence,
And fever followed at His feet.
⁶ He stood and measured the earth;
He looked and startled the nations.
And the everlasting mountains were scattered,
The perpetual hills bowed.
His ways *are* everlasting.
⁷ I saw the tents of Cushan in affliction;
The curtains of the land of Midian trembled.
⁸ O Lord, were *You* displeased with the rivers,
Was Your anger against the rivers,
Was Your wrath against the sea,
That You rode on Your horses,
Your chariots of salvation?
⁹ Your bow was made quite ready;
Oaths were sworn over *Your* arrows.[b] *Selah*
You divided the earth with rivers.
¹⁰ The mountains saw You *and* trembled;
The overflowing of the water passed by.
The deep uttered its voice,
And lifted its hands on high.
¹¹ The sun and moon stood still in their habitation;
At the light of Your arrows they went,
At the shining of Your glittering spear.
¹² You marched through the land in indignation;
You trampled the nations in anger.
¹³ You went forth for the salvation of Your people,
For salvation with Your Anointed.
You struck the head from the house of the wicked,
By laying bare from foundation to neck. *Selah*

¹⁴ You thrust through with his own arrows
The head of his villages.
They came out like a whirlwind to scatter me;
Their rejoicing was like feasting on the poor in secret.
¹⁵ You walked through the sea with Your horses,
Through the heap of great waters.
¹⁶ When I heard, my body trembled;
My lips quivered at *the* voice;
Rottenness entered my bones;
And I trembled in myself,
That I might rest in the day of trouble.
When he comes up to the people,
He will invade them with his troops.
¹⁷ Though the fig tree may not blossom,
Nor fruit be on the vines;
Though the labor of the olive may fail,
And the fields yield no food;
Though the flock may be cut off from the fold,
And there be no herd in the stalls—
¹⁸ Yet I will rejoice in the Lord,
I will joy in the God of my salvation.
¹⁹ The Lord God[c] is my strength;
He will make my feet like deer's *feet,*
And He will make me walk on my high hills."

Jehoshaphat Prays for Deliverance from the Enemy

"Then Jehoshaphat stood in the assembly of Judah and Jerusalem, in the house of the Lord, before the new court,⁶ and said: "O Lord God of our fathers, are You not God in heaven, and do You not rule over all the kingdoms of the nations, and in Your hand is there not power and might, so that no one is able to withstand You? ⁷ Are You not our God, who drove out the inhabitants of this land before Your people Israel, and gave it to the descendants of Abraham Your friend forever? ⁸ And they dwell in it, and have built You a sanctuary

in it for Your name, saying, ⁹ 'If disaster comes upon us—sword, judgment, pestilence, or famine—we will stand before this temple and in Your presence (for Your name is in this temple), and cry out to You in our affliction, and You will hear and save.' ¹⁰ And now, here are the people of Ammon, Moab, and Mount Seir—whom You would not let Israel invade when they came out of the land of Egypt, but they turned from them and did not destroy them— ¹¹ here they are, rewarding us by coming to throw us out of Your possession which You have given us to inherit. ¹² O our God, will You not judge them? For we have no power against this great multitude that is coming against us; nor do we know what to do, but our eyes are upon You."

Other Example of Righteous Prayers that God has Answered and will Answer

Prayer of Jabez

1 Chronicles 4:10 "And Jabez called on the God of Israel saying, *"Oh, that You would bless me indeed, and enlarge my territory, that Your hand would be with me, and that You would keep me from evil, that I may not cause pain!"* So God granted him what he requested.

Pray with a Contrite Spirit

Luke 18:13
"God, have mercy on me, a sinner." Luke 18:13

Jeremiah 14:7

"Although our iniquities testify against us, O Lord, act for Thy name's sake! (Jeremiah's Prayer)

Pray by Praising, Glorifying, and Exalting God's name

1 Samuel 2:1-2

" *My heart rejoices in the Lord; my horn is exalted in the Lord…No one is holy like the Lord, for there is none besides You, Nor is there any rock like our God".*

Daniel 4:3

"It has seemed good to me to show the signs and wonders that the Most High God has done for me. How great are His signs, how mighty His wonders! His kingdom is an everlasting kingdom, and His dominion endures from generation to generation." (King Nebuchadnezzar's Prayer)

Pray with a Humble Spirit

Judges 16:28 "O Lord God, please remember me and please strengthen me…" (Samson's Prayer)

Pray with Faith

Matthew 8:2 "Lord, if You are willing, You can make me clean."
(The Leper's Prayer)

**Mathew 21:22 also teaches us that when you ask
believing, they will be answered.**

Jonah 2:1-9
"I called out of my distress to the Lord, and He answered me. I
cried for help from the depth of Sheol; You heard my voice."
(Jonah's Prayer)

2 Chronicles 14:11
"Lord there is no one besides You to help in the battle
between the powerful and those who have no strength; so
help us our God, for we trust in You and in Your name..."
(Asa's Prayer)

Prayers that Confirm our Authority to Perform Signs and Wonders

Acts 4:29-30

"Now Lord, look on their threats, and grant to Your servants
that with all boldness they may speak Your word, by stretching
out Your hand to heal, and that signs and wonders may be
done through the name of Your holy Servant Jesus."

Mark 16:17-18

"And these signs will follow those who believe: In My name they will cast out demons; they will speak with new tongues; they will take up serpents; and if they drink anything deadly, it will by no means hurt them; they will lay hands on the sick, and they will recover."

Prayers for times of fear, trouble and/or Protection

Psalm 23

The Lord *is* my shepherd; I shall not want.
² He makes me to lie down in green pastures;
He leads me beside the still waters.
³ He restores my soul; He leads me in the paths of righteousness
For His name's sake.
⁴ Yea, though I walk through the valley of the shadow of death,
I will fear no evil; For You *are* with me;
Your rod and Your staff, they comfort me.
⁵ You prepare a table before me in the presence of my enemies;
You anoint my head with oil; My cup runs over.
⁶ Surely goodness and mercy shall follow me
All the days of my life;
And I will dwell in the house of the Lord Forever."

Psalms 27: 1-3

"The Lord is my light and my salvation—whom shall I fear?
The Lord is the stronghold of my life—of whom shall I be afraid?
When evil men advance against me to devour my flesh,
when my enemies and my foes attack me,
they will stumble and fall.
Though an army besiege me, my heart will not fear;

though war break out against me, even then will I be confident."

God Stores all our prayers in heaven!

Our prayers are precious to the Lord and not one is lost. The cries and prayers of the saints throughout this age, and of those who are martyred because of their testimony of the Lord Jesus, is the main reason for the great tribulation. When God's elect are pursued and persecuted it provokes the wrath of God into vindication mode. This is why God unleashes the judgments upon a fallen world during the coming apocalypse - just before the return of Messiah Jesus.

Revelation 8:1-4

"When He opened the seventh seal, there was silence in heaven for about half an hour. ² And I saw the seven angels who stand before God, and to them were given seven trumpets. ³ Then another angel, having a golden censer, came and stood at the altar. **He was given much incense, that he should offer** *it* **with the prayers of all the saints** *upon the golden altar which was before the throne.* **⁴ And the smoke of the incense, with the prayers of the saints, ascended before God from the angel's hand***."*

NOTE: You can better understand the **mysteries of Revelation** and the **coming apocalypse** by getting a copy of my new release **"Revelation Mysteries Decoded: Unlocking the Secrets of the Coming Apocalypse"**

Chapter 4 - Praying for Healing

"And God shall wipe away all tears from their eyes;
and there shall be no more death,
neither sorrow, nor crying,
neither shall there be any more pain:
for the former things are passed away." **Revelation 21:4**

Sickness is a consequence of original sin – prior to that there was no sickness. God does not want us to be sick. Jesus died to allow us to be healed physically and spiritually. But sometimes healing does not come this side of heaven.

It seems like most people don't reach out to God, except when they are in need of healing or some other need. Well human selfishness aside, let's explore the bible for God promises of healing.

The bible offers many verses on healing. Healing comes from the Holy Spirit. God can give you back your health and even restore back time for you that may have been lost due to illness. In the book of **Joel 2:25** God teaches that he can *"repay you for the years the locusts have eaten..."*. In other words he can restore time lost due to illnesses or any other trials of life!

Let me premise the fact that God and the word can heal by saying that it requires faith and also that when God says it is time to go home, it is time.

Healing comes in different ways such as dipping in water, mud in eyes, by a shadow, by intersession **James 5:14-15**, via handkerchiefs; anointing in oil, laying of hands, and sometimes just by praying.

In the book of **Isaiah Chapter 38:1,** we learn that King Hezekiah, who had much faith in the Lord, fell sick and Isaiah received a message from God to tell King Hezekiah to get his house in order because he was going to die and was not going to recover from that illness.

Well Hezekiah despite this certain message of death from both God and the great prophet Isaiah, prayed and wept bitterly for healing **(Isaiah 38:2-3)**. He cried about how unfair his affliction was given all his years of service to God. Merciful God heard his prayer, and commanded Isaiah to tell King Hezekiah the following: "....*I have heard your prayer and seen your tears; I will add 15 years to your life.*" God also defended his city which was being attacked by the Assyrians **(Isaiah 38:4-6)**.

The passage above should inspire all of us to never surrender to illness!

We should pray persistently and bind the power of the spirit of sickness and disease. **You see, God gets glory when we prosper in health and in all areas of life. The word reveals that by his stripes we are healed.**

The God who created all things including doctors, and hospitals, created miracle *healings*! **And when he created man, he made us in his image, so that we might be empowered to heal ourselves and others if we so claim that empowerment.** We can even be Gods instruments of healing for others, if God imparted in you the gift of healing others, and if not - pray for it! All of us were born with God given gifts, such as writing, prophecy, teaching, and of course healing. There are approximately 17 gifts that the bible refers to - and all of us have at least one!

There are so many souls out there who need healing. Some are in great physical pain; others need emotional healing. As the salt of the earth, we can reach out to them and heal their pain, or at least pray for their healing. We can invoke the power that God instilled in all of us when he created us in his image. ***But first of course, let's use that power to heal ourselves!***

5 Ways to Ensure Healing from Sickness and Illness

1) **Stay immersed in the word of God**. Focused on the word. Occupy your mind not with the symptoms, but with the healing that you
will receive through faith and the word! **Proverbs 4 vs 20-22 says**: [20] "My son, pay attention to what I say; turn your ear to

my words. [21] Do not let them out of your sight, keep them within your heart; [22] for they are life to those who find them *and health (healing) to one's whole body."*

2) **Reconcile with God**. Ask God for forgiveness of all sin in your life – consecrate yourself in preparation for healing.

3) So that healing can manifest itself faster, *keep the word in your heart* – so it can become an enshrining heart in God's eyes.

4) **Claim God's will and promise of healing**, and believe with faith.

5) **Have your family, friends and church members pray for your healing**. Even if you have no family or friends, in his mercy, God still provides for you! There are many Christian help lines throughout the world that you can call, and they will pray with you for your healing.

Now you may not receive an answer to your prayer(s) instantly, but through prayer, faith, perseverance and patience you eventually will! That is what the word promises and what faith is all about!

Below are a few verses that offer proof that spiritual healing is available for all who believe and claim healing:

Psalm 107 vs. 20 teaches us that healing comes from the word.

Luke 10:19: "Behold I give unto you power to tread on

serpents and scorpions, and over all the power of the enemy, and nothing shall by any means hurt you".

Luke 9:1-7; "When Jesus had called the Twelve together, _**he gave them power and authority**_ _**to drive out all demons**_ _**and to cure diseases,**_ 2 and he sent them out to proclaim the kingdom of God _**and to heal the sick**_. 3 He told them: "Take nothing for the journey—no staff, no bag, no bread, no money, no extra shirt. 4 Whatever house you enter, stay there until you leave that town. 5 If people do not welcome you, leave their town and shake the dust off your feet as a testimony against them." 6 So they set out and went from village to village, proclaiming the good news _**and healing people everywhere**_.
Yes, **God gave us Power and Authority over all Illness** (Luke 9:1)! All we have to do is to believe and claim this authority! The 12 apostles are symbolic of all future Christians; all those believers in Jesus Christ are granted this Power and Authority! This is why the Gospel is called "The Good News"!

Why is God Not Healing Me or My Loved One?

The power of the Holy Spirit moves in weakness, sickness, and a broken spirit. Perhaps that is why God calls the sinner, the downcast, the downtrodden (as opposed to the proud) to repentance and to serve him in his ministry!

In moments of weakness we become more sensitive to God's inner voice and we are more inclined to listen to Him. We become more humble, more patient, and perhaps even kinder and more loving.

God sometimes delays healing because He needs us to straighten our spiritual life. He may also be trying to get our attention, or to strengthen our faith, character or spiritual fortitude. *God may be testing our faith*, by making us wait for our healing. *Perhaps God is arranging to put us in touch with someone empowered with the gift of healing*.

Sometimes during a period of protracted illness we draw closer to God by prayer and reading his word. *Sadly for many, they never reach out to God except when they need healing or some other thing from God....as if God is their servant; role reversal at its worst!*

The main reason many do not receive healing is because they do not have faith. We must claim God's will and promise of healing, and *believe with faith, and then we can be healed!* It may not be today or tomorrow, but because of your faith - *in God's timing...*you will receive healing! *After all what is faith? Faith is all about waiting on God for our needs*, such as healing.

By the way, there is no reason to NOT seek medical attention whenever we need healing. After All, in His mercy, God has made provisions for even those without or with little faith to receive healing. ***God uses Doctors and hospitals as instruments of physical healing for both those with and those without faith***. And of course there are chronic illnesses that require immediate and or ongoing medical attention. But it cannot hurt to add faith into the healing picture - it is like the icing on the cake!

God provides much more than just physical healing - God provides spiritual, and emotional healing as well. God heals those who suffer and are heartbroken. ***God can heal us from anything.***

Other Reasons that Some People do not receive Healing

1) **Insufficient instruction and knowledge** of, nor faith in the healing power of the bible; the word of God.

2) **Lack of United prayer** (where everybody in the room believes in the power of healing of God).

3) **Community unbelief** (see Mark chapter 6 vs. 4-6). When a community or a nation do not believe in God nor follow the word, there will be few healing miracles for those who live there. Read Mark 6:4-6 "Jesus said to them, "A prophet is not without honor *except* in his own town, among his relatives and in his own home." [5] ***He could not do any miracles there,***

except lay his hands on a few sick people and healing them. [6] He was amazed at their lack of faith."

4) **Traditions and misperceptions of mankind**, such as the misguided belief that "sickness is the will of God", or that "the age of healing and miracles has past". Some even believe that it is not God's will to heal us all!

5) **They break natural laws**. They abuse their body (they smoke, drink, take drugs, eat unhealthy, etc.).

6) **Lack of faith** in God's healing power.

7) **Unresolved sin** and **un-forgiveness** in your heart/life. A primary example which proves that healing is God's will is when we read the life of Jesus. ***Jesus spent most of his short time on earth healing the sick***! He healed the sick as the son of God, the perfect representative of God's will for us. God does indeed promise healing, and these promises are referenced in many places in the bible.....

Even More Passages regarding God's promises for healing

<u>Genesis 20:17</u> Abraham prayed and God healed Abimilek. We learn here that Abraham did not have the gift of healing but he prayed for healing!

Luke 9:1-2"When Jesus had called the Twelve together, he gave them power and authority to drive out all demons and to *cure diseases*, and he sent them out to proclaim the kingdom of God and to heal the sick.

Proverbs 4 vs. 20-22 Teaches us that we can be healed by reading the word of God: "My son, pay attention to what I say; turn your ear to my words. Do not let them out of your sight, keep them within your heart; for they are life to those who find them and *health (healing) to one's whole body*."

Exodus 23:25 God will remove sickness from those who worship him.

Jeremiah 30:17 God promises to restore us to health and to heal our wounds. *Please remember that although these promises were to Israel in this example - they pertain to all who read and embrace these words from God!*

Psalm 107:20 God heals through his word in the bible.

Isaiah 53:4-5 We are healed by Jesus death at the cross. By his stripes we are healed.

Mark 6:4-6 teaches us that when a person or community does not have faith, he/they cannot be healed by God: "Jesus said to them, "A prophet is not without honor except in his own town, among his relatives and in his own home." He could not do any miracles there, except lay his hands on a few sick people and healing them. *He was amazed at their lack of faith*."

Luke 10:19 *teaches us that God's promises go beyond just physical healing:*"Behold I give unto you power to tread on serpents and scorpions, and over all the power of the enemy, and nothing shall by any means hurt you".

Jesus ministry while here on earth was full of many examples of healing.

Since we are to be and do like Jesus than we too must have been empowered to heal. The following promise by Jesus should clearly bring that message home:

Mark 16:17-18 *"And these signs will follow those who believe: In My name they will cast out demons; they will speak with new tongues; they will take up serpents; and if they drink anything deadly, it will by no means hurt them; they will lay hands on the sick, and they will recover."*

In **Mathew 13:57-58** we learn that ***Jesus did not heal some because of their lack of faith***. So, obviously the law of faith is crucial in order to unlock the power of prayer and receive our answers, or miracle.

God promises healing, for all those who believe that they can be healed or that they can heal others in Jesus name! Indeed, God gave us Power and Authority over all Illness (**Luke 9:1**)! All we have to do is to believe and claim this authority!

So don't stop praying, don't lose hope. Just be patient and confident in your faith.......your day of healing may come at any time.

Expanded List Healing Verses:

- **Jeremiah 17:14**

- **James 5:16 confess our sins first**

- **2 Corinthians 1:20**

- **James 5:14-15**

- **Romans 8:11**

- Mark 16:18

- Jeremiah 32:27

- Exodus 23:25-26

- Psalm 21:4; Psalm 42:11; Psalm 103:2-3

- Jeremiah 30:17

- Proverbs 4:20-22

- 2 Chronicles 20:22

- Exodus 15:26

- Numbers 23:19

- Deuteronomy 5:33 and 7:11-15 and 30:19-20

- 2 Chronicles 16:9; 30:20

- Job 37:23

- Psalm 32; 34:19; 41:3; 91:10-16; 103:2-3; 105:37; 107:20; 147:3

- Proverbs 3:1-2; Proverbs 3:7-8; 4:20-22; 9:11; 14:30; 16:24

- Isaiah 40:29; 40:31; 41:10; 53:4-5; 55:11; 58:8

- Jeremiah 17:14; 30:17

- Malachi 3:6; 4:2

- Mathew 4:23-24; 7:11; 8:2-3; 8:5-13; 8:14-17; 9:20-22; 9:27-35; 10:1; 10:7-8; 11:2-5; 12:15; 14:13-14; 14:34-36; 15:29-31; 18:19-20; 19:1-2; 21:14; 24:35

- Mark 1:32-34; 2:1-12; 5:21-43; 6:5-6; 6:53-56; 10:46-52; 11:23-24; 16:15-20

- Luke 4:16-21; 4:40; 6:6-10; 7:11-16; 9:1-2, 6-11; 10:8-9

- John 5:2-14; 9:1-7; 10:10; 14:13-14; 15:7; 16:23-24

- Acts 3:1-8; 5:12; 5:16; 8:5-8; 9:33-34; 10:38; 14:8-10; 19:11-12

- Romans 4:19-21; Romans 8-11; Romans 8:32

- 1 Corinthians 6:20; 12:7-11; 28

- Ephesians 6:1-3

- 1 Thessalonians 5:23-24

- Hebrews 4:14-16; 10:23; 10:35-36; 11:1; 11:6; 13:8

- James 1:17; 5:14-16

- 1 peter 2:24

- 1 John 5:14-15

- 3 John 1;2

How to Pray for Supernatural Healing

*Hebrews 12:13...and make straight paths for your feet, so that what is lame may not be dislocated, but rather **be healed**.*

Prayer is very powerful because the spoken word is very powerful. Words can be spoken for the good or for bad. We will all encounter a disease or illness sometime in our life. Below are some powerful prayers that you can use to pray for yourself or others.....

Powerful healing Prayers - for General and Specific Illnesses

"In the name of Jesus, I take authority over this sickness and disease and I command it to die, dissipate and disappear from (the person's) body now - be healed in the name of Jesus"
"Lord I forgive everybody including myself"

"Father in the name of Jesus, in the power of that name, let your anointing flow through my hands, I declare by the stripes

of Jesus that I have received healing in Jesus Holy name, by my faith in the name and in the blood of Jesus, I claim and receive your healing right now". **Now confidently repeat** *(as many times as you wish): "The power of God is working in me, and I thank God that I have received healing."*

Arthritis

"In the name of Jesus I speak to the demonic power giving life to this person's body, I call you out, and I command the pain and the reason for the pain in Jesus name - go NOW".
Hip Pain: "Father, I speak miracles of healing into each hip right now in the name of Jesus be healed, be well"

Back Pain/slipped disk (slipped Disc/spine problem - for a NEW disk):

"In the name of Jesus I suspend time, I command the old disk to disappear, I call form the 3rd heaven a brand new disk, let it be put in her body now, I command the pain and the reason for the pain to go now, I speak to the spine - be healed...3,2,1.."
"Father touch his back, let the pain and reason for the pain literally fade away."

Shorter leg/heal Scoliosis

"In the name of Jesus, you dark power giving light to scoliosis, come out of his/her body, Lord let her leg grow, I command this spine to grow into place now in Jesus name" "It is written by his stripes and by his wounds you are healed"

Eye Diseases

"In the name of Jesus I curse these eye diseases, die, dissipate and disappear from their bodies, I command Glaucoma _____ disappear, be gone and stay gone, I command total restoration of the eye now, In Jesus name.

Weight Loss/Overweight

"Father let the angels take their position, Father *I release your power of kingdom healing.* I know that power comes out of the glory, I hereby command the miracle of supernatural weight loss into (name) in Jesus name for your glory"

Metal in the Body

"In the name of Jesus I suspend time, I speak to the metal in your body, I command you to disappear, Lord let the angel go get the bone to take its place and put in his body now, and I command that bone be physically created in his leg now, and I command the pain and the reason for the pain in Jesus name go now." 3 2, 1 tell me when all the pain is gone.

" In the name of Jesus I call for a rotator cup to be created in this man's shoulder now, I command the pain and the reason for the pain - go now"

A Prayer Courtesy of David and Barbara Cerullo

I would like to also share the following prayer courtesy of David and Barbara Cerullo. You can replace the spaces provided below with your name or with the name(s) of the person(s) you are praying for....

"Father we come before you today in the name of Jesus – we thank you Lord Jesus that you paid the price for our healing and that by your stripes we are healed – we thank you Father that we have the right to come before you and to appropriate your healing power in _____ life. We know Lord you get no honor from the sickness or poverty of your children, but that you get honor when your children are blessed and prospering and healthy because it reveals to the world your glory and your power and your righteousness, and what a great Father we serve.

So Father we come before you now and in the name of Jesus we rebuke any spirit of disease and sickness that has afflicted _____. We rebuke every work of the curse that would come against _____ mind, body and against _____ spirit.

Every spirit of infirmity, we command you Satan and spirits of sickness of disease not in our name but in the name of Jesus Christ, and in the authority of the word of God, we command your spirits of disease to be released from _____ body NOW - Father in the heavens we ask that you bind the powers and principalities of the enemy and rebuke the enemy that comes against _____ with sickness and disease in the heavens for you said that you will bind in heaven what we bind in earth and you would lose in heaven what we lose on earth. So Father right now we speak healing over_____ we say to you now by the stripes of Jesus _____ is healed.

Right now let the healing virtue of Jesus Christ flow through _____ body and make _____ 100% whole in Jesus name – be healed in the name of Jesus.

Father in the heavens we ask you to release your spirit of healing – let your ministering angels go right now and minister healing to _____. To their body, mind emotions, spirit. Minister your healing to their family and broken relationships and every area of their life. In the Name of Jesus, I thank and praise you and bless your name because you are God almighty and there is none other – and your power can conquer all. We thank you God the Almighty in the name of Jesus of Nazareth, AMEN!

"Father let the angels of healing take their position. I release your power of kingdom healing. I know that power comes out of your glory. I hereby command the miracle of supernatural weight loss into my (or the person's name) in Jesus name for your glory, amen"

For multiple afflictions, you can continue as follows

…"I further speak for a miracle of healing of this (name the illness) for (your or the person's name) to be healed right now in the name of Jesus"

For supposed irreparable illness (such as missing limbs, slipped disks, Scoliosis, or whatever), you can pray as follows.....

"In the name of Jesus I suspend time, I command this (name the infirmity) to disappear, I call from the 3rd heaven a brand new (name the organ or whatever is damaged or missing), let it be put in your/his/her body now. I command the spirit of pain and the reason for the pain to be healed right now. I command all side effects thereof to leave right now in Jesus name, amen."

A Prayer For Those Facing Death

Those who face life threatening illnesses, and their loved ones, at some point need to consider offering up to God; a prayer of gratitude for the gift of life. And at all times it is appropriate to release a loved one into the hands of God. For those approaching what may be the end of life, I offer this:

"God of compassion and love, you have breathed into us the breath of life
and have given us minds and bodies in which we live out our days on earth.
For the gift of life, we are grateful.

*We humbly acknowledge that there is a time to live, and a
time to die.
We commit this life to you, trusting in your gracious promises
and
confident in the sure and certain hope of new life in the world
to come.
Into your hands we commit our beloved. May your will be
done!
In the good and gracious name of Christ, we pray. Amen."*

Other sample healing prayers:

*"Heavenly father, in the name of Jesus and in the power of
that name; let your anointing flow through my hands. I declare
by the stripes of Jesus that I have received healing in Jesus
Holy name, by my faith in the name and in his blood, I claim
and receive your healing right now".* ***Now confidently
repeat*** *(as many times as you wish): "The power of God is
working inside of me, and I thank God that I have received
healing."*

NOTE: You should pray in your own words following the
above outlines. ***Your own style for communicating to the
Creator is precious to his ears!*** God gave us each our own
unique spirit so he will listen to us when we speak from our
heart! The key is that you pray in faith and in expectation to
receive an answer.

Should we seek medical help or advice, or would this compromise our faith in healing?

Yes, we should always seek medical help when we suffer from chronic illness or disease. Who created medicine? Man did not create doctors or medicines, God did! And out of God's love and mercy, he blessed and enabled many gifted people to create and invent healing medicines and procedures! The problem is that many people do not want to give credit to God for anything. Yet when they get sick or ill, many immediate reject God because of their suffering and blame him for all of their ills!

But while we are receiving medical attention, *it can only help expedite the entire healing process - if we immerse ourselves in prayer for rapid healing.* This faith in spiritual healing will perhaps make the medication work even better and faster for you! *It is like the icing on the cake of healing*, if you will!

In closing out this chapter, let me pray for you...

  "Heavenly father God, I pray for all those souls that are currently enduring pain, suffering and illness in their life. I pray that the healing power of the Holy Spirit and the sanctified blood of Jesus manifest itself in them and heal them right now. I pray that all who believe, that by their faith they are quickly healed; that through their healing they may serve as a witness to those whom they encounter throughout their life. I pray that those that they heal may also harness your kingdom power; so that this healing miracle spreads like an uncontrollable virus and heal millions more. We thank you Lord as we witness your healing in our lives and in the lives of our loved ones; we worship your glory Lord and glorify almighty God in heaven, Amen"

Chapter 5 - Inspirational Bible Prayer Passages

"Therefore I say unto you, what things so-ever ye desire, when ye pray, **believe that ye receive them***, and ye shall have them." ***Mark 11:24**

1 Samuel 12:23 "Moreover as for me, God forbid that I should sin against the LORD in ceasing to pray for you: but I will teach you the good and the right way"

2 Samuel 22:4 "I will call on the LORD, who is worthy to be praised: so shall I be saved from mine enemies."

Job 22:27 "Thou shall make thy prayer unto him, and he shall hear thee, and thou shall pay thy vows."

1 Chronicles 16:11 "Look to the LORD and his strength; seek his face always."

1 Chronicles 16:13 "O ye seed of Israel his servant, ye children of Jacob, his chosen ones."

2 Chronicles 7:14 "If my people, which are called by my name, shall humble themselves, and pray, and seek my face, and turn from their wicked ways; then will I hear from heaven, and will forgive their sin, and will heal their land."

Psalm 4:1 - "Answer me when I call to you, O my righteous God. Give me relief from my distress; be merciful to me and hear my prayer."

Psalms 5:3 "My voice shalt thou hear in the morning, O LORD; in the morning will I direct my prayer unto thee, and will look up."

Psalms 9:12 "When he makes inquisition for blood, he remembers them: he forgets not the cry of the humble."

Psalms 18:6 In my distress I called upon the LORD, and cried unto my God: he heard my voice out of his temple, and my cry came before him, even into his ears.

Psalms 21:2 "Thou hast given him his heart's desire, and hast not withheld the request of his lips. Selah."

Psalms 34:15 "The eyes of the LORD are upon the righteous, and his ears are open unto their cry."

Psalms 34:17 "The righteous cry, and the LORD hears, and delivers them out of all their troubles."

Psalms 37:4 "Delight thyself also in the LORD; and he shall give thee the desires of thine heart."

Psalms 38:15 "For in thee, O LORD, do I hope: thou wilt hear, O Lord my God."
Psalms 40:1 I waited patiently for the LORD; and he inclined unto me, and heard my cry.

Psalms 40:2 He brought me up also out of a horrible pit, out of the miry clay, and set my feet upon a rock, and established my goings.

Psalms 40:3 And he hath put a new song in my mouth, even praise unto our God: many shall see it, and fear, and shall trust in the LORD.

Psalms 42:8 Yet the LORD will command his loving kindness in the daytime, and in the night his song shall be with me, and my prayer unto the God of my life.

Psalms 50:15 And call upon me in the day of trouble: I will deliver thee, and thou shall glorify me.

Psalms 51:10 Create in me a clean heart, O God; and renew a right spirit within me.

Psalms 55:17 Evening, and morning, and at noon, will I pray, and cry aloud: and he shall hear my voice.

Psalms 55:22 Cast thy burden upon the LORD, and he shall sustain thee: he shall never suffer the righteous to be moved.

Psalms 62:8 Trust in him at all times; ye people, pour out your heart before him: God is a refuge for us. Selah.

Psalms 66:18 If I regard iniquity in my heart, the Lord will not hear me:

Psalms 66:19 But verily God hath heard me; he hath attended to the voice of my prayer.

Psalms 86:7 In the day of my trouble I will call upon thee: for thou wilt answer me.

Psalms 91:15 He shall call upon me, and I will answer him: I will be with him in trouble; I will deliver him, and honor him.

Psalms 107:6 Then they cried unto the LORD in their trouble, and he delivered them out of their distresses.

Psalms 107:13 Then they cried unto the LORD in their trouble, and he saved them out of their distresses.

Psalms 107:19 Then they cry unto the LORD in their trouble, and he saves them out of their distresses.

Psalms 107:28 Then they cry unto the LORD in their trouble, and he brings them out of their distresses.

Psalms 116:4 Then called I upon the name of the LORD; O LORD, I beseech thee, deliver my soul.

Psalms 118:5 I called upon the LORD in distress: the LORD answered me, and set me in a large place.

Psalms 119:13 With my lips have I declared all the judgments of thy mouth.

Psalms 130:2 Lord, hear my voice: let thy ears be attentive to the voice of my supplications.

Psalms 138:3 In the day when I cried thou answers me, and strengthened me with strength in my soul.

Psalms 140:6 I said unto the LORD, Thou art my God: hear the voice of my supplications, O LORD.

Psalm 145:18 "The LORD is near to all who call on him, to all who call on him in truth."

Psalms 145:19 "He will fulfill the desire of them that fear him: he also will hear their cry, and will save them."

Proverbs 8:17 I love them that love me; and those that seek me early shall find me.

Proverbs 15:8 The sacrifice of the wicked is an abomination to the LORD: but the prayer of the upright is his delight.

Proverbs 15:29 The LORD is far from the wicked: but he hears the prayer of the righteous.

Proverbs 18:24 A man that hath friends must show himself friendly: and there is a friend that sticks closer than a brother.

Isaiah 26:3 Thou wilt keep him in perfect peace, whose mind is stayed on thee: because he trusts in thee.

Isaiah 28:23 Give ye ear, and hear my voice; hearken, and hear my speech.

Isaiah 40:31 But they that wait upon the LORD shall renew their strength; they shall mount up with wings as eagles; they shall run, and not be weary; and they shall walk, and not faint.

Isaiah 55:6 Seek ye the LORD while he may be found, call ye upon him while he is near:

Isaiah 58:9 Then shall thou call, and the LORD shall answer; thou shall cry, and he shall say, Here I am. If thou take away from the midst of thee the yoke, the putting forth of the finger, and speaking vanity;

Isaiah 59:2 But your iniquities have separated between you and your God, and your sins have hid his face from you, that he will not hear.

Isaiah 65:24 And it shall come to pass, that before they call, I will answer; and while they are yet speaking, I will hear.

Jeremiah 29:11 For I know the thoughts that I think toward you, says the LORD, thoughts of peace, and not of evil, to give you an expected end.

Jeremiah 29:12 Then shall ye call upon me, and ye shall go and pray unto me, and I will hearken unto you.

Jeremiah 29:13 And ye shall seek me, and find me, when ye shall search for me with all your heart.

Jeremiah 33:3 Call unto me, and I will answer thee, and show you great and mighty things, which thou knows not.

Ezekiel 22:30 And I sought for a man among them, that should make up the hedge, and stand in the gap before me for the land, that I should not destroy it: but I found none.

Matthew 5:44 But I say unto you, Love your enemies, bless them that curse you, do good to them that hate you, and pray for them which despitefully use you, and persecute you;

Matthew 6:5 And when you pray, thou shall not be as the hypocrites are: for they love to pray standing in the synagogues and in the corners of the streets, that they may be seen of men. Verily I say unto you, they have their reward.

Matthew 6:6 But thou, when thou prayest, enter into thy closet, and when thou hast shut thy door, pray to thy Father which is in secret; and thy Father which seeth in secret shall reward thee openly.

Matthew 6:7 But when ye pray, use not vain repetitions, as the heathen do: for they think that they shall be heard for their much speaking.

Matthew 6:8 Be not therefore like unto them: for your Father knows what things ye have need of, before ye ask him.

Matthew 6:9 After this manner therefore pray ye: Our Father which art in heaven, Hallowed be thy name.

Matthew 6:10 Your kingdom come. Yours will be done in earth, as it is in heaven.

Matthew 6:11 Give us this day our daily bread.

Matthew 6:12 And forgive us our debts, as we forgive our debtors.

Matthew 6:13 And lead us not into temptation, but deliver us from evil: For Yours is the kingdom, and the power, and the glory, forever. Amen.

Matthew 7:7 Ask, and it shall be given you; seek, and ye shall find; knock, and it shall be opened unto you:

Matthew 7:8 For every one that asks receives; and he that seeks finds; and to him that knocks it shall be opened.

Matthew 7:11 "If you, then, though you are evil, know how to give good gifts to your children, how much more will your Father in heaven give good gifts to those who ask him!"

Matthew 16:19 And I will give unto thee the keys of the kingdom of heaven: and whatsoever thou shall bind on earth shall be bound in heaven: and whatsoever thou shall loose on earth shall be loosed in heaven.

Matthew 17:20 And Jesus said unto them, Because of your unbelief: for verily I say unto you, If ye have faith as a grain of mustard seed, ye shall say unto this mountain, Remove hence to yonder place; and it shall remove; and nothing shall be impossible unto you.

Matthew 17:21 Howbeit this kind goes not out but by prayer and fasting.

Matthew 18:18 Verily I say unto you, Whatsoever ye shall bind on earth shall be bound in heaven: and whatsoever ye shall loose on earth shall be loosed in heaven.

Matthew 18:19 Again I say unto you, That if two of you shall agree on earth as touching anything that they shall ask, it shall be done for them of my Father which is in heaven.

Matthew 18:20 For where two or three are gathered together in my name, there am I in the midst of them.

Matthew 21:21 Jesus answered and said unto them, Verily I say unto you, If ye have faith, and doubt not, ye shall not only do this which is done to the fig tree, but also if ye shall say unto this mountain, Be thou removed, and be thou cast into the sea; it shall be done.

Matthew 21:22 And all things, whatsoever ye shall ask in prayer, believing, ye shall receive.

Mark 9:29 And he said unto them, this kind can come forth by nothing, but by prayer and fasting.

Mark 10:27 And Jesus looking upon them says, with men it is impossible, but not with God: for with God all things are possible.

Mark 11:17 And he taught, saying unto them, is it not written, My house shall be called of all nations the house of prayer? but ye have made it a den of thieves.

Mark 11:24 Therefore I say unto you, what things so-ever ye desire, when ye pray, believe that ye receive them, and ye shall have them.

Mark 11:25 And when ye stand praying, forgive, if ye have aught against any: that your Father also which is in heaven may forgive you your trespasses.

Mark 11:26 But if ye do not forgive, neither will your Father which is in heaven forgive your trespasses.

Luke 6:12 "One of those days Jesus went out to a mountainside to pray, and spent the night praying to God."

Luke 11:9 And I say unto you, Ask, and it shall be given you; seek, and ye shall find; knock, and it shall be opened unto you.

Luke 11:10 For every one that asks receives; and he that seeks finds; and to him that knocks it shall be opened.

Luke 11:11 If a son shall ask bread of any of you that is a father, will he give him a stone? or if he ask a fish, will he for a fish give him a serpent?

Luke 11:12 Or if he shall ask an egg, will he offer him a scorpion?

Luke 11:13 If ye then, being evil, know how to give good gifts unto your children: how much more shall your heavenly Father give the Holy Spirit to them that ask him?

Luke 18:1 And he spoke a parable unto them to this end, that men ought always to pray, and not to faint;

Luke 21:36 Watch ye therefore, and pray always, that ye may be accounted worthy to escape all these things that shall come to pass, and to stand before the Son of man.

Luke 18:1 "Then Jesus told his disciples a parable to show them that they should always pray and not give up."

John 3:27 John answered and said, A man can receive nothing, except it be given him from heaven.

John 10:27 My sheep hear my voice, and I know them, and they follow me:

John 14:13 And whatsoever ye shall ask in my name, that will I do, that the Father may be glorified in the Son.

John 14:14 If ye shall ask any thing in my name, I will do it.

John 15:5 I am the vine, ye are the branches: He that abides in me, and I in him, the same brings forth much fruit: for without me ye can do nothing.

John 15:7 If ye abide in me, and my words abide in you, ye shall ask what ye will, and it shall be done unto you.

John 15:16 Ye have not chosen me, but I have chosen you, and ordained you, that ye should go and bring forth fruit, and that your fruit should remain: that whatsoever ye shall ask of the Father in my name, he may give it you.

John 16:23 And in that day ye shall ask me nothing. Verily, verily, I say unto you, Whatsoever ye shall ask the Father in my name, he will give it you.

John 16:24 Hitherto have ye asked nothing in my name: ask, and ye shall receive, that your joy may be full.

Acts 2:42 May I be devoted "to the apostles' instruction and the communal life, to the breaking of bread and the prayers".

Acts 6:4 But we will give ourselves continually to prayer, and to the ministry of the word.

Acts 16:25 And at midnight Paul and Silas prayed, and sang praises unto God: and the prisoners heard them.

Acts 16:26 And suddenly there was a great earthquake, so that the foundations of the prison were shaken: and immediately all the doors were opened, and every one's bands were loosed.

Romans 8:13 May I "put to death the works of the flesh by yielding to the Spirit"

Romans 8:26 Likewise the Spirit also helps our infirmities: for we know not what we should pray for as we ought: but the Spirit itself makes intercession for us with groans which cannot be uttered.

Romans 12:12 Rejoicing in hope; patient in tribulation; continuing instant in prayer;

Philippians 4:6 "Do not be anxious about anything, but in everything, by prayer and petition, with thanksgiving, present your requests to God."

Colossians 1:9 May I "attain full knowledge of His will through perfect wisdom and spiritual insight"
Colossians 1:10 May I "lead a life worthy of the Lord and pleasing to Him in every way"

Colossians 1:11 May I "be endowed with the strength needed to stand fast, even to endure joyfully whatever may come" (Col 1:11).

Colossians 4:2 "Devote yourselves to prayer, being watchful and thankful."

1 Corinthians 2:9 But as it is written, Eye hath not seen, nor ear heard, neither have entered into the heart of man, the things which God hath prepared for them that love him.

Ephesians 3:20 Now unto him that is able to do exceeding abundantly above all that we ask or think, according to the power that works in us,

Ephesians 5:20 Giving thanks always for all things unto God and the Father in the name of our Lord Jesus Christ;

Philippians 2:9 Wherefore God also hath highly exalted him, and given him a name which is above every name:

Philippians 4:6 Be careful for nothing; but in everything by prayer and supplication with thanksgiving let your requests be made known unto God.

Philippians 4:7 And the peace of God, which passes all understanding, shall keep your hearts and minds through Christ Jesus.

Philippians 4:13 I can do all things through Christ which strengthens me.

1 Thessalonians 5:17 "pray continually;"

1 Thessalonians 5:16-18 "Rejoice always; pray without ceasing; in everything give thanks; for this is God's will for you in Christ Jesus."

1 Timothy 2:8 "I want men everywhere to lift up holy hands in prayer, without anger or disputing."

Hebrews 4:14 "Therefore, since we have a great high priest who has gone through the heavens, Jesus the Son of God, let us hold firmly to the faith we profess."

Hebrews 4:16 Let us therefore come boldly unto the throne of grace, that we may obtain mercy, and find grace to help in time of need.

Galatians 5:24 By the Spirit may I crucify the flesh and not stifle the Spirit.

James 1:7 "That man should not think he will receive anything from the Lord;"

James 1:17 Every good gift and every perfect gift is from above, and cometh down from the Father of lights, with whom is no variableness, neither shadow of turning.

James 4:3 You ask, and receive not, because ye ask amiss, that ye may consume it upon your lusts.

James 4:8 Draw nigh to God, and he will draw nigh to you. Cleanse your hands, ye sinners; and purify your hearts, ye double minded.

James 5:13 Is any among you afflicted? let him pray. Is any merry? let him sing psalms.

James 5:15 And the prayer of faith shall save the sick, and the Lord shall raise him up; and if he have committed sins, they shall be forgiven him.

James 5:16 Confess your faults one to another, and pray one for another, that ye may be healed. The effectual fervent prayer of a righteous man avails much.

James 5:17 Elijah was a man subject to like passions as we are, and he prayed earnestly that it might not rain: and it rained not on the earth by the space of three years and six months.

James 5:18 And he prayed again, and the heaven gave rain, and the earth brought forth her fruit.

1 Peter 3:12 For the eyes of the Lord are over the righteous, and his ears are open unto their prayers: but the face of the Lord is against them that do evil.

1 Peter 5:7 Casting all your care upon him; for he cares for you.

1 John 1:9 "If we confess our sins, he is faithful and just and will forgive us our sins and purify us from all unrighteousness"

1 John 3:21 Beloved, if our heart condemn us not, then have we confidence toward God.

1 John 3:22 And whatsoever we ask, we receive of him, because we keep his commandments, and do those things that are pleasing in his sight.

1 John 5:14 And this is the confidence that we have in him, that, if we ask any thing according to his will, he hears us:

1 John 5:15 And if we know that he hear us, whatsoever we ask, we know that we have the petitions that we desired of him.

Other Powerful Prayer Examples in the Bible

Old Testament

Abraham's Intercession for Sodom & Gomorrah **Genesis 18:23-33**

Hezekiah's Prayer when Sick - **Isaiah 38:2-8**

King Hezekiah's Prayer for the nation - **2 Kings 19:15-19**

Daniel's Prayer for the Captive Jews - **Daniel 9:4-19**

The Prayer of Jabez - **1 Chronicles 4:10**

David's Prayer for Protection **Psalm 3**

David's Prayer of Thanks - **2 Samuel 7:18-29**

David's Prayer for Favor **Psalm 4**

David's Prayer for Guidance **Psalm 5**

David's Prayer for Mercy **Psalm 6**

David's Prayer from Persecution **Psalm 7**

David's Prayer for God's Help **Psalm 13**

David's Prayer For Trust **Psalm 25**

David's Prayer For Forgiveness **Psalm 51**

Elijah's Prayer for the Widow's Son **1 Kings 17:20-22**

Elijah's Prayer at Mt. Carmel **1 Kings 18:36-39**

Esther's Prayer for Israel **Esther 4 & 5; Ezra 8:21-23**

Hannah's Prayer for a Child **1 Samuel 1:10-12**

Hannah's Prayer of Thanksgiving **1 Samuel 2:1-10**

Jacob's Deliverance from Essau **Genesis 32:9-12**

Jacob At Peniel **Genesis 32:24-30**

Jehoshaphat prayer for deliverance **2 Chronicles 20**

Moses Intercession for the Children of Israel **Exodus 32:11-13 32:31-32 33:12-13 Exodus 33:18**

Moses Intercession For Miriam **Numbers 12:13**

Moses & the Promised Land **Deuteronomy 3:24-29**

Moses & Israel **Deuteronomy 9:26-29**

Moses' 40 Day Prayer **Deuteronomy 9:18-20; 9:25-29**

Nehemiah's Prayer **Nehemiah 1:3-11;** 9:1
Samson's prayer **Judges 16:28**

Solomon's Prayer to Dedicate the Temple **1 Kings 8:23-61**

New Testament

Jesus temptation **Matthew 4:1**

Jesus Praying in the Wilderness **Matthew 6:6**

The Lord's Prayer **Matthew 6:9-13 & Luke 11:2-4**

Jesus Prayer to the Father **John 12:27-28**

Jesus Prayer of Thanksgiving **Matthew 11:25-26**

Jesus Praying in Gethsemane **Matthew 26:39 & 42**

Jesus Prayer at the Cross **Luke 23:34, 46; Matthew 27:46**

Apostles Prayer for Divine Direction **Acts 1:24,25**

The Apostles & Believer's Prayer **Acts 4:24-31**

Stephen's Prayer at His Stoning - **Acts 7:59-60**

Cornelius Prayer **Acts 10:30-31**

Early Church Prayer **Acts 13:1-3**

Paul Prayer for the Corinthians **2 Corinthians 13:7**

Paul's Prayer for Spiritual Wisdom - **Ephesians 1:15-23**

Paul's Prayer to the Ephesians for Spiritual Growth - **Ephesians 3:14-21**

Paul's Prayer to the Philippians for Partners in the Ministry - **Philippians 1:3-11**

Paul's Prayer to the Colossians for Knowing God's Will - **Colossians 1:9-17**

A Prayer of Praise - **Jude 1:24-25**

Chapter 6 - Prayers for a Job, Blessings, or Anything Else

"And whatever you ask in My name, that I will do, that the Father may be glorified in the Son.
If you ask anything in My name, I will do it." **John 14:13-14**

In this chapter I provide sample prayers for different needs other than health, which was already covered in a prior chapter. Let us begin with praying for a job and continue from there.

Learn How to Correctly Pray for That "Perfect Job

What the Bible Teaches us about How we Should Pray for a Job, Health or Anything……

When we pray, we are in direct communication with our creator God almighty. So we need to be careful on how we pray and what we ask for, and how we ask. If we pray with the right frame of mind, we will receive our answer. If we pray with frustration, anger, and we demand quick results, well you should know how far that will take you! Every word that we pray is recorded in Heaven forever (Revelations). Jesus our Lord, said that if we had the faith of a mustard seed, then we could move mountains (**Revelation 8:3-4**).

Because of God's gift to us to decide how we wish to live out our life, God rarely intervenes, so he needs our prayer/authority to intervene in our lives.

Jesus promised us that when we ask anything (obviously anything that is good and in accordance with God's plans for our life - such as a job), that we will receive it. **John 14:13-14**

Based on these promises, we can be at peace recognizing that if it is good for us, God will hear and answer our prayer. Is it good for us to find a job, or to be healed of an illness? Of course it is. So we need to pray earnestly and in faith knowing that God will answer your prayers at the right time, the appointed time.

I believe that we at times do not get our answer as quickly as we want to, but let's understand that the Lord will answer our prayer, but he will answer it in accordance with God's timetable, not ours.

Many people pray and then stop praying within days, due to impatience or lack of faith. They may have prayed just short of having received God's blessing!

To find a job or the answer to any prayer, the Bible teaches us to pray constantly and meditate regularly for the job. We must pray constantly for the job because we cannot expect to ask for something just once and we will immediately receive it. We must learn to "Wait" on the Lord.

We live in an instant gratification society, and we all want it "Now". Well that won't happen when it comes to prayer! God wants the best for us, so that when we pray for a job with patience, God will search for that "PERFECT" job for us.

God may even influence employers and even alter situations to make it happen, so that the "perfect job" may eventually fall right on your lap. After all, God knows about every job out there, he knows every employer out there and job seeker too - whether we know him or not, God is the most influential person in the Universe! You most definitely want God on your side, when seeking a job ;)

Of course you can't just sit back in your Lazy chair and expect the employers to call you. You must earnestly seek out that job, always praying and meditating on God's word and promises. When you run into a job that you want, you will pray with faith earnestly for that job, and if it is good for you, God will most likely respond.

Persistence and Repetition is good, when it come to praying for a job or anything else that we need. God wants us to ask repeatedly, he will never tire from hearing our faithful prayers. After all, when we are searching for a job we do not just send out 1 resume, we send out many, many and sometimes even many more. But persistence will eventually lead to great results.

This chapter will not discuss how to prepare for an interview, that is beyond the scope of this message. However, as an owner of a company that has interviewed many job hunters, let me just add some Key tips for you:

1) On the initial call do NOT ask for job specifics, especially NOT about the salary, hours of work, benefits, etc.
2) Dress Your Best for that type of position.
3) Ask intelligent questions.
4) research as much you can about the Company, the job, the interviewer.
5) Be on time, offer a firm handshake, maintain a positive and confident disposition. Smile throughout, and speak with a clear and energetic voice.
6) Do not bad mouth your prior employer(s).
7) Role play the interview, and the types of questions you may be asked.

How Should We Pray for a Job or Anything We Need?

1) We must pray with a grateful and thankful heart.
2) We must pray for the right job persistently.
3) We must meditate daily with prayer and the word for our answer.
4) We must pray with faith, expecting that God will answer our prayer.
5) Never pray with the wrong frame of mind such as lack of faith, with anger, frustration, impatience.
6) God's word and promises in the Bible is his will so we do not need to pray "Lord if it is your will. This only limits results - since it is in the word than it is God's will, period! John 5 Vs. 14
7) Your prayer should be built and established upon the word of God. We need to master the words of the bible relative to prayer, so that we can unlock the maximum blessings that result when we pray correctly!

By the way, you should pray to God just like you should conduct yourself and your words in the midst of a job interview! You are alert, respectful, upright, confident and enthusiastic, meditating on every "word" the interviewer says; you exude confidence, positivity, and with a spirit of expectancy. How much more when we pray to our creator - should we do so with these positive attributes!

Praying for Other Needs

As already discussed, when we pray we are in direct communication with our creator God almighty. So we need to be careful on how we pray and what we ask for, and how we ask. *If we pray with the right frame of mind, we will receive our answer.* If we pray with frustration, anger, and expecting an instant solution, well you should know how far that will take you - and it certainly will NOT lead to your answer or blessing.

Based on the many promises throughout the bible, evidenced by the many verses that we already listed in this book, you can confidently expect that if it is good for you, God will hear and answer your prayer. So understanding this, we should all *pray earnestly, confidently and boldly in faith* knowing that God will answer our prayers at the right time - which is *His appointed time.*

Of course, God is the one who determines if it is good for us, since only God knows our destiny here on earth and for eternity. Only the Lord has the power to grant us eternal life, and He does not take that lightly. Sometimes God will nudge us a bit to get us back on track and sometimes He will allow a major calamity in our life in an effort to save our soul. Love at times forces discipline.

Ask God to Guide Your Life

When we submit to the Lord, it is like the trust we place on an airplane pilot or a ship's captain. We have faith that this person is more qualified than we are to safely land the plane or steer the ship and to get us to our desired destination as quickly as possible!

How much more "faith" then should we place in omnipotent God to be the Captain of our life and destiny. To try to navigate our ship of life by ourselves is like navigating a ship or flying a plane with blinders on!

You can find this prayer at the close of the last chapter of this book.

Praying to Resist Temptation

"Lord, strengthen the Holy Spirit in me that I may resist the temptations of Satan, in Jesus name I pray, Amen."

Prayer to be Like Father Jesus

"Lord God, thank you for the Holy Spirit, please strengthen the Holy Spirit in me so that I can replace my sinful carnal mind with the Love, character and personality of Jesus Christ, in Jesus name I pray, Amen."

Prayer before reading the Bible

"Lord God, as I prepare to read your divine word, please bless me with your Spirit of wisdom and open my eyes and mind so that I may understand your message for me in the Bible. In Jesus name I pray, Amen."

Prayer for Forgiveness and Salvation

"Lord God, please forgive me for my sins and have mercy on my soul; that I may be found worthy to enter your Kingdom at the appointed time, so that I may be raptured on the day that you rapture, and that I may be sheltered on the day of your anger."

Prayer for Protection against Evil

Lord, please protect us from all the evils and evil peoples of this world; from demons and principalities, antichrist and false prophet(s), so that they do not steal, vandalize, harm or destroy me and my loved ones, in Jesus Holy name I pray, Amen."

Praying for Wealth or Financial Security

"Lord God in the name of Jesus I believe your word that Jesus was made poor so that we may be made rich, he has completed his work, and I receive that completed work, I declare by the word of God that I am made rich. I receive an anointing for wealth and a war chest and in the name of Jesus the Angels are released to go and bind the strongman, to plunder his house and bring me the spoils. In the name of Jesus I am not a thief; I tithe and give and as a result I am qualified to receive wealth, it comes to me now in the name of Jesus."

Prayer to Serve the Lord

"Heavenly Father I am available to be used by the Holy Ghost for intercession. Use me, my vocal chords, my mouth, and my life to show mercy and compassion upon whomever you desire, in Jesus name I pray, Amen"

Prayer for the BLESSING of Abraham:

"Heavenly father, now that you have released the power of genetic salvation in my life, by releasing me from the power of the corrupted genetic inheritance of my forefathers, through the completed work of the Messiah on the cross. So I now release my faith towards experiencing the blessing of Abraham in my life."

Prayers of Praise to the Lord

"Heavenly Father, creator of the universe - creator of all things, I thank you Lord for the blood of Jesus, thank you that because of the blood of Jesus I can call you Father, I can pray to you Father. Thank you that by the blood of Jesus I have a blood bought right to come boldly before the throne of God and to ask for help in my time of trouble; I have the wisdom of God, the Righteousness of God, I have been sanctified, and redeemed. Thank you that I now have a blood bought right to have the ever presence of the Holy Spirit, wholeness in my spirit, soul and body. I Thank you that I now have a blood bought right to all of the New Testament promises, and to get answers to all of my prayers, in Jesus name I thank you heavenly father, Amen"

Prayer to Change Your DNA and inherit Christ's Bloodline

The following prayer is presented courtesy of **Francis Myles**, author of **"Breaking Generational Curses"**. According to Francis, this powerful prayer can be recited to repair spiritually damaged DNA!

"Heavenly Father, I stand in your royal courtroom; to receive your righteous judgment over my bloodline inheritance.

Heavenly Father, I call upon your holy angels to be witnesses to this legal and righteous transaction, as well as enforce the righteous decree of this royal court; over my life.

Heavenly Father, I also decree and declare that all the demonic powers which have been attached to the bloodline of my natural ancestors - will respect and honor your righteous judgment over my genetic inheritance.

Heavenly Father your word says that if we confess our sins, you are faithful and just to forgive our sins and clearance us from all unrighteousness.
Heavenly Father, forgive me for worshipping my family ancestry instead of giving it up for Messiah my Lord.

Heavenly Father I willingly and joyfully denounce the (family name) lineage. I denounce the lineage that this name represents and all the demonic anomalies and iniquities that are attached to it through the timeline of this lineage. It can no longer affect my destiny. I hereby give it up to possess Christ's Holy and flawless prophetic bloodline.

Heavenly Father I willingly and joyfully denounce the (family name) lineage. I denounce the lineage that this name represents and all the demonic anomalies and iniquities that are attached to it through the timeline of this lineage. It can no longer affect my destiny. I hereby give it up to possess Christ's Holy and flawless prophetic bloodline.

Heavenly Father I willingly and joyfully denounce any and all superimposed DNA over my life arising from witchcraft, sexual assault, faulty blood transfusions, adoption, trauma, mind control, and sexual immorality.

I strongly denounce all of the demonic anomalies, and iniquities that are attached to this superimposed DNA; and declare that this superimposed DNA can no longer interfere with my destiny in the Messiah. I give up any association with this superimposed DNA in order to possess Christ's holy and flawless prophetic DNA.

Heavenly father, as I now prepare to jump over the prophetic bloodline, I release my faith for the healing of my body and all genetic anomalies, in Christ's name I pray.

Heavenly father, as I now prepare to jump over the prophetic bloodline, I release my faith for the healing of my body and all genetic anomalies, in Jesus Christ's name I pray. In the name of the Lord Jesus Christ I jump

(Now jump over a makeshift line which can be a ruler, rope or belt, etc.)
- Then shout: "thank you Lord Jesus and God the Almighty, Praise the Lord, Glory to God the Almighty"

Chapter 7 - Things that we should Never PRAY for

"So now I, the Lord, warn them that I am going to bring destruction on them, and they will not escape.
And when they cry out to me for help, I will not listen to them.*"*
Jeremiah 11:11

If you've ever had the experience of praying for something and receiving no clear answer, it's natural to wonder whether or not God heard the prayer in the first place. Did He ignore the prayer? Should God's silence be taken as a "No" answer?

The good news is that the Bible doesn't leave us wondering. Many bible passages and prayer samples give us a way to measure the integrity of our heart and our request, so as to determine the likelihood that God will hear or answer us. And when we do approach God earnestly, we can rest confidently on this bible promise: "***The prayer of the righteous person is powerful in what it can achieve***."

James 5:16
*"Confess your trespasses to one another, and pray for one another, that you may be healed. **The** effective, fervent **prayer of** a **righteous** man avails much."*

So let's start off with things that we should not pray for.

1) Do Not pray to be "Perfect"

Do not pray *"to be good or sinless"*. Rather, pray **to be righteous and Holy**. To allow the Holy Spirit to help you resist temptation, is better and easier than to try to be sinless on your own.

100

David knew he was a sinner and understood this important concept, he asked God to renew in him a renewed mind through the spirit of God (**Psalm 51:10**). This is the mindset that we all must have. This is what leads to a greatly blessed life.

2) Do Not Pray to be Rich

- Do not pray to become rich or wealthy when we are living a life of lust for money - it will NOT be answered. And even if you do achieve great wealth on your own, it is crucial that you do not substitute money for God. In the end, the money stays and you will go before the Lord. The amount of money you accumulated during your stay on earth, is not a criteria that God uses to judge out spiritual character. However the level of lust for money that we had, will count as a negative! During our stay on earth is the time to get our priorities right.

Instead of lusting for money, pray that God can open doors of provision so that you can pay your bills and feed your family, and be debt free. The former is based on greed while the latter is based on trying to be a responsible human being free of debt.

3) Do Not Pray for Others to be Harmed

- Do not pray that others would be harmed because of a wrong that they did to you or your loved one. Rather, pray that God will convict their soul. The former is based on anger, hatred and revenge while the later is based on allowing God to convict that person's soul so that perhaps, through Gods conviction and not ours, that person may change their ways and perhaps someday also receive the gift of salvation. Vengeance belongs to the Lord.

God is LOVE and so it is so difficult for many of us to allow others who have hurt us to be forgiven. We fail to remember the greatest commandment - to love our neighbor as ourselves. So when we sin and hurt others, do we ask God to hurt us because of our transgressions? So therefore neither should we desire punishment for others. When we forgive others and allow God to exact His righteous judgment, you are demonstrating to God that you understand who is in charge; that we are all sinners and when we forgive, we will be forgiven. God does not need our help, that is why vengeance belongs solely to the LORD! We need to let go and let God. Do NOT play God!

The world is full of hatred, and heaven is full of love (total opposites). There is no room in heaven for hatred. Sometimes I watch these documentaries of parents who lost their child to murderers. I am so humbled by how perfectly some parents understand the concept of LOVE by forgiving the perpetrator. They know that ONLY God, who is void of hatred, can righteously convict and exact judgment on those who have shed the blood of a loved one. There are many sins that are hidden on earth - and they will all be unveiled on the day of judgment.

There is no greater blessing for the mind, body and soul than to have a spirit of LOVE; for only love can forgive, and only Love can get us to heaven. The mind of the person who forgives because of love, is the mind that is full of peace. All sin evolves from hatred and or selfishness. Heaven is a place of perpetual Love and Joy, and this is why sinners cannot make it to heaven. It is not that God is unfair or cruel, it is because God is pure love and righteousness and paradise therefore is TOTALLY void of sin and filth. That is why God gives all of us MANY opportunities to repent while on earth.

Christianity and the opportunity for salvation could never have happened if one of the greatest haters of Jesus and the followers of Jesus was not forgiven by Jesus Himself - that man was called Saul of Tarsus (St. Paul) - who once smitten by the Love of the Lord, became the greatest and bravest

102

evangelist for the cause of Christianity; for Jews and gentiles alike.   Never condemn your brother - who knows that he or she may eventually see the light and save millions of souls as the apostle Paul did! This is why "vengeance belongs to the Lord".

Yes, God many times may test us by making us endure pain and suffering for many years. Yet He never tests us beyond the capacity of our spirit. He is refining our spirit and soul. It is NOT because God wants to make us suffer, but rather that He wants us to prove our faith in Him. And our reward in heaven will be greater because of our perseverance. We will all receive a crown in heaven, but there are special crowns for those who endure beyond the level that most can endure. As Revelation reveals, there will be many kings and Priests in heaven. This may be why Jesus is not referred to as the King, but rather the "*King of Kings*".

4) Only Pray for what is Spiritually Pure

Never pray for anything that is not spiritually pure. God will not deliver anything to us that is not spiritually good for us, or that is not in accordance with Gods plans for our life. Rather when you pray, always ask for it only "if it is in His will for our life".

I believe that if the enemy cannot get into our mind first, with evil and sinful thoughts - then he cannot attack us with illness in our body.

When does God Refuse to Hear Prayers?

Now that I have covered some things to not pray for, let's explore why sometimes we do not seem to get an answer for a righteous request (i.e. healing). Most of us believe that when we "cry out" to God—that is, appeal to Him through prayer—He always hears those prayers. "Ask," we read

in *Matthew 7:7*, "and it will be given to you."
There are however passages that indicate that sometimes
God ignores certain prayers?

In *Psalm 66*, in which the author gives thanks that God
answered his prayer, but suggests that God might not have
done so in certain circumstances:

Psalm 66:16-20

"Come and hear, all you who fear God,
and I will tell what he has done for my soul.
I cried to him with my mouth,
and high praise was on my tongue.
If I had cherished iniquity in my heart,
the Lord would not have listened.
But truly God has listened;
he has attended to the voice of my prayer.
Blessed be God,
because he has not rejected my prayer
or removed his steadfast love from me!"

In Jeremiah 11, God warns a backslidden nation that
He *won't* listen to their cries:
*"So now I, the Lord, warn them that I am going to bring
destruction on them, and they will not escape. And when they
cry out to me for help, I will not listen to them."* **Jeremiah
11:11**

1) When it's Too Late

In the case of the passages above, judgment had already been passed, and so it was too late for repentance. The nation of Judah had disobeyed God's laws and ignored his pleas repeatedly over many years, and so judgment was already bestowed upon the land and its people. **God told Jeremiah not to pray for the people (Isaiah 14:11–12),**

The same will happen during the Apocalypse when at that point it will be too late for mankind to repent and to delay the "*day of the Lord's Anger*" (also referred to as **the great tribulation**). For more information on this coming time of great trouble, get a copy of my new release *"Revelation Mysteries Decoded: Unlocking the Secrets of the Coming Apocalypse"*.

2) When we are living in sin

The message above is clear; that if we are living in sin, and not repentant, then God will NOT listen to our prayers. Since God sees, hears and knows everything, He can measure the level of sincerity in our heart, so He knows what our real motives are behind our words.

3) A Compromised Prayer Life

If there is unresolved conflict between you and your neighbor (includes family), or a wrong that you have committed, this will hinder your prayer life.

It's also possible that *people sometimes compromise their own prayers*. The Bible does make it clear that there are certain things that can nullify our prayer life:

1) Asking for Something that is not in God's will for us
2) Disobedience (see Pr 28:9)
3) Insincerity of heart or hypocrisy (see Isa 29:13; Mal 1:7–9)
4) lack of faith (Heb 11:6; Jas 1:6)
5) Transgressions/sin (see Ps 66:18; Isa 59:2; Jer 14:10–12)
6) The wrong motive (see Mt 6:5–6; Lk 18:11–14; Jas 4:3)
7) Unresolved conflict, Marital or Family problems (see 1Pe 3:7)

What sometimes appears to be no answer to prayer may actually be the answer itself, or a delayed answer (**see Dan 10:12–13**). **God may be denying our request in order to give us something better than what we knew to ask for, and he is waiting for us to discover that truth**.

So yes there may be times when our prayers will be ineffective, but I believe that if we are in sync with our spirit, in those times the spirit will make us feel deep inside that this particular request is not in God's will, or will not be heard. This is why it is important to sharpen our spiritual ear so that we can hear what the Spirit is telling us.

There are times when our prayers are futile, but I believe that if we are in sync with our spirit, in those times the spirit will make us feel deep inside that this particular request is not in God's will. This is why it is important to sharpen our spiritual ear so that we can hear what the Spirit is telling us.

Chapter 8 - The Prayer of Salvation

"And when he came to the den, he cried out with a lamenting voice to Daniel. The king spoke, saying to Daniel, "Daniel, servant of the living God, whom you serve continually, been able to deliver you from the lions?"
Then Daniel said to the king, "O king, live forever! **My God sent His angel and shut the lions' mouths, so that they have not hurt me, because I was found innocent before Him**; *and also, O king, I have done no wrong before you."* **Daniel 6:20-22**

There are so many precious souls in this world right now, who are enduring great pain and suffering. I can almost guarantee you that many of these are also the kindest and sweetest people that you will ever meet. Although they may endure great suffering here on earth, their reward will be GREAT in heaven. There are many types of crowns (positions) reserved in heaven, and as Father Jesus promised us: *"The First will be Last, and the Last will be First"* Matthew 19:30

When you feel like all hope is gone, remember that you are God's child, and He loves you even more than our earthly loved ones could ever love you. The love of your parents, children, siblings and spouse are just a tiny example of the immense love that emanates from the very essence of our Heavenly Father. The love and joy that exists in heaven is beyond the scope and capacity for our earthly mind and soul to take in!

Unlike mortal man, God does not play games with our emotions and our wellbeing. God always delivers His faithful children, at His appointed time. And when God blesses, He blesses us more than we ever expected or than we ever deserved. *So our perseverance in prayer is well worth the wait!* And the longer we faithfully wait for our answer - the greater the reward will be!

Because He is so patient with all of us sinners, God rewards the faithful and the patient. That is why throughout the bible we learn that most of the patriarchs had to patiently wait for their blessings.

Here are just 2 quick example:

1) Moses and the Israelites had to wander the desert for 40 years (a period of consecration) before entering the promised land.

2) Abraham faithfully waited to the age of 100 before God delivered His promise of the covenant child (Isaac).

Because of Abraham's patience and faithfulness, it would be through his and his descendant's seed that the Messiah Christ would become a man, that through Christ's shed blood all the peoples and all the nations of the world have been blessed!

When God promises Paradise - He means Paradise! We get just a small sample of the Glory of Heaven in **Revelation chapter 21 and 22**. Again, I must emphasize that the full Glory of heaven is beyond the capacity for our mortal senses to fully appreciate!

As the earth unravels in the soon coming apocalypse, be reassured in knowing that God's love conquers all. While the world grows in hatred and iniquity, you will grow in love because unlike the lost of the world, you know what awaits you on the other side, and you are too wise to let go of that glorious opportunity.

Because of your faith in the Lord, you will persevere in these last days, by immersing yourself in the word, and by constant communication with the Lord. When the enemy attempts to attack you with panic attacks and his other fiery darts, he will not be able to afflict you because, just like Daniel in the Den of Lions **(Daniel 6:20-22),** your prayers, and faith will protect you. You are further protected because you know how to put on the "full armor of God" in accordance with (**Ephesians 6:11-18).** God's angels protect His elect; you are His elect when you accept God as the Captain of your ship!

Fear including the fear of the unknown, can no longer torment you, because you know that God's Angels protect His elect. God has assigned an Angel over you. You are His elect when you accept God as the Captain of your ship (your life)!

I pray that this book inspires you to communicate with the Lord in a more fervent, consistent, and intimate manner, so that you too can unlock supernatural heavenly blessings upon you and your loved ones. That through your faithful prayers, you will become closer to the almighty, and reap the blessings thereof. I pray that as you grow closer to the Lord that you may enjoy the peace and joy that you and your loved ones deserve.

The Prayer of Salvation

The prayer of salvation is the greatest opportunity that we will ever have in our very short time in this great green earth, to secure our salvation. And we only have to pray it once (but the more the better)!

As your fellow servant signs out, pray the following prayer of salvation with me...

*"Awesome Heavenly Father, I worship and praise your Holy Name. You are **the God of Abraham, Isaac, and Jacob** -*

the Supreme God of the Universe. I minister unto you thanksgiving for all of your goodness; I praise you for delivering me from all evils. You are the great God; Mighty, Strong, Loving, Patient and Perfect in every way. You are Abba God the Almighty and there is none other than You! I lift up my hands in adoration, and I say Halleluiah to the Almighty Creator of the universe. I say Halleluiah to the Almighty King, for you are his Majesty, the King; my Rock; my Fortress. You are the great Jehovah; You are the most high God, for whom is like unto thee? **Nobody!**

There is no one and nothing in the universe greater than you God - for You are everything and I am nothing outside of you; indeed nothing can exist outside of You! Father I am here today to humbly repent of all my present and past sins and to say thank You for forgiving, saving and delivering me through the blood of the Lamb Jesus Christ, my Savior and my Redeemer.

You are my breath of life and my heartbeat, my healer, and my hope. I submit my soul and my life to you right now, and all the days of my life. Be the Captain of my life. I hereby let go of the controls today, and allow You to take control of my destiny and to steer my ship safely to its final port of call - the port at **Salvation***, Paradise and Eternal Life. You are my* **Salvation** *Lord God, and to that end I am yours.*

I give you my life and my thanks Oh Holy God, in Jesus Name, Amen.*"*

Get Complimentary Access to: "Prophecy Alerts"

Dear Reader: Prophecies are being fulfilled so rapidly in these last days that I am offering my readers complimentary access to "***prophecy alerts***" so that you get "***Breaking Prophecy News***" as soon as it breaks...Just follow this link below and sign Up today...
http://robertritebooks.com/prophecy-alerts/

Note:
If you do not have a Bible you can benefit from online sources such as this fantastic resource "**Bible Gateway**": *http://www.biblegateway.com/*

If you found this book enlightening, would you please share this message with others as follows:

1) Like our page at www.facebook.com/RobertRiteBooks

2) Tweet "I recommend reading books @Robert Rite

3) Right a review on amazon.com or goodreads.com

4) Consider reading my other books

5) Visit my blog that hosts many articles at: http://bible-blog.org

Related Books by Robert Rite

"Awaken the Supernatural You!"

"Aliens, Fallen Angels, Nephilim and the Supernatural"

"Be healed!...How to Unlock the Supernatural Healing Power of God"

"Revelation Mysteries Decoded - Unlocking the Secrets of the Coming Apocalypse"

"Signs in the Heavens - Divine Secrets of the Zodiac & the Blood Moons of 2014"

Available at Amazon and other distribution channels

About The Author:

Robert Rite is the author of six spiritual and supernatural based books including:

- "Revelation Mysteries Decoded"
- "Signs in the Heavens, Divine Secrets of the Zodiac & the Blood Moons of 2014!"
- "Aliens, Fallen Angels, Nephilim and the Supernatural",
- "Be healed!....How to Unlock the Supernatural Healing Power of God"
- "Awaken the Supernatural You!"
- Over 100 articles on the word of God and related non-fiction publication.

Most recently Robert has released "Signs in the Heavens: Divine Secrets of the Zodiac & the Blood Moons of 2014!" which is part of the "Supernatural Series" of books. These are the first in a series of inexpensive non-fiction works planned for release in the near future.

Robert is also the creator of bible-blog.org where he has written over 135 articles on bible facts, and end-of-day prophecies among other related topics. Other books and properties are planned to be released starting in 2014; all will be non-fiction in nature with subject matters that really matter, such as health, money management, success and related.

With over 25 years experience in the marketing, management, publishing, and sales field, and as President and CEO of a successful company, Robert has a lot to share with the online and offline community with digital based and physical books and related publications.

www.ingramcontent.com/pod-product-compliance
Lightning Source LLC
Chambersburg PA
CBHW070520030426
42337CB00016B/2030